formula
MATH
METAL FABRICATORS and WELDERS
John R. Martel BSc B.Ed.

Welder/Metal Fabricator (Fitter)

Blocks 1-3 Math Review

By John R Martel BSc B.Ed.

Introduction

'Why don't you write a math book?' is a question I get asked quite often. This always made me think, why don't I? When I first started teaching, I simply had no time, and content books seemed to be available. Then technology advanced, and it became possible to carry volumes of information and apps to do your work for you all in the palm of your hand on a mobile device/phone.

Yet, it still seemed to be important. No book exists that explains the math skills required to pass the Red Seal math exam for welders and steel fabricators. Until now. The intent then of this handbook is to be a review of the concepts that you would have covered during the 3 blocks of training that you have gone through to get to this point. It is not a true textbook. It is a handbook, a summary of the skills already learned with some problems to practice and bring those skills back up to a point where you can write the exam with some confidence.

This book then needed to be written and so now I can tell my students past, present, and future that I have, in fact, written a textbook. And it is only available on that mobile device that we all seem to carry around these days, so it is accessible at all times, compact, and easy to carry.

This was created with Microsoft Word, Paint and MathType over several versions as this was a work that spanned several years.

Dedication

I dedicate this mathematical handbook to my mother who has always believed in me, especially during my difficult times. She is a rock who worked tirelessly making sure to wring the full meaning from the word 'Mom'.

I also wish to recognize my wonderful wife whose contribution to this text was quite significant. She edited all the text and kept me from looking bad. Trust me, my literature skills are nowhere close to my mathematical skills.

Cover Art Credit

The fantastic cover was designed by a great friend of ours, Steve Ethier. He was an accomplished and loved fellow instructor who has authored many (many) AutoCAD texts and runs his own energy blog. His list of accomplishments is phenomenal and I am humbled by his gift of this great cover.

Contents

Place Values

123456789.9876543

100 millions
10 millions
millions
100 thousands
10 thousands
thousands
hundreds
tens
ones
tenths
hundredths
thousandths
10 thousandths
100 thousandths
millionths
10 millionths

This is easier to read in the table below.

Place Name	Digit
Hundred millions	1
Ten millions	2
Millions	3
Hundred thousands	4
Ten thousands	5
Thousands	6
Hundreds	7
Tens	8
Ones	9
DECIMAL PLACE	.
Tenths	9
Hundredths	8
Thousandths	7
Ten thousandths	6
Hundred thousandths	5
Millionths	4
Ten Millionths	3

Addition and Subtraction of Whole and Decimal numbers

Addition

Whole Numbers

Line up the numbers by the place values and add.

1.

123
+45
168

2. with carrying

$6\ 3^{1}5^{1}8$
$+\ 499$
6857

The tiny '1's are the carry values

Decimal numbers – line up the numbers by their decimal points and add.

1.

$123^{1}.8^{1}7$
$+\ 1.984$
125.854

The space after the 7 was filled with a zero as a place holder.

Subtraction

This is done the same as the addition as far as lining up the numbers. Instead of carrying values, there may be borrowing from the 'neighbour' to the left.

$^{5}\not{6}\ ^{12}\not{3}\ ^{14}\not{5}\ ^{1}8$
$-\ \ \ 4\ \ 9\ 9$
5 8 5 9

Use the same principle on the decimal numbers.

Multiplication and Division of Whole and Decimal Numbers

```
 123
x54
  492    123x4
 6150    123x50
 6642    add the two lines above
```

The zero on the fourth line down is a place holder for the ones place and is necessary to keep all the numbers lined up in their proper places.

Decimals

Multiply as if the decimals don't exist and then in your final answer move the decimal the same number of places as the total number of places in the problem.

```
  0.123     3 decimal places
 x0.54      2 decimal places
    492
   6150
0.06642     5 decimal places
```

Division

Whole numbers

The statement $24 \div 4$ **is read as 24 divided by 4. This is then rewritten as** $4\overline{)24}$ **.**

The '4' is known as the divisor and the 24 is known as the dividend.

$$\frac{\text{divisor}}{\text{dividend}} = \frac{\text{numerator}}{\text{denominator}} = \frac{\text{top number}}{\text{bottom number}} = \text{bottom number}\overline{)\text{top number}}$$

The next method simplifies long division by hand and is called the 'double division method'.

Here are some examples on the next page.

$27\overline{)4018}$	**Write down 1x, 2x, 4x, and 8x with answers by the 27**
1x $27\overline{)4018}$ 2x 54 4x 108 8x 256	**From the list pick a value that is less than the 40**
1x $27\overline{)4018}$ 2x 54 <u>2700</u> 100 4x 108 8x 256	**Subtract the values. The '100' to the right stands for 1 times and the zeros needed.**
1x $27\overline{)4018}$ 2x 54 <u>2700</u> 100 4x 108 1318 8x 216 <u>1080</u> 40 238 <u>216</u> <u>8</u> 22 148R22	**This is continued until the last number is smaller than the divisor "27". The values on the right are added up and including the remainder are the answer to the question.**
$\frac{4018}{27} = 27\overline{)4018} = 148R22 = 148\frac{22}{27}$	

Here is another one without the explanations.

$1x35 = 35$	$35\overline{)9397}$	
$2x35 = 70$	<u>7000</u>	200
4x35=140	2397	
8x35=280	<u>1400</u>	40
	997	
	<u>700</u>	20
	297	
	<u>280</u>	<u>8</u>
	17	268R17 ← Answer

If you wanted to calculate the decimal places as well, start with a new division using the remainder and the same divisor. If you want 3 decimal places accuracy, calculate out to 4 places and round off. To show the 4 place accuracy, 4 zeroes will be added to the remainder.

The next example continues where the last one stopped.

$$35\overline{)\;9397}^{\,268R17}$$

$1x35 = 35$	$35\overline{)170000}$	
$2x35 = 70$	$\underline{140000}$	4000
4x35=140	30000	
8x35=280	$\underline{28000}$	800
	2000	
	$\underline{1400}$	40
	600	
	$\underline{350}$	10
	250	
	$\underline{140}$	4
	110	
	$\underline{70}$	2
	40	
	$\underline{35}$	$\underline{\quad 1}$
	5	4857=0.4857

so $35\overline{)9397} = 268 + 0.4857 = \underline{\underline{268.486}}$

The method above is intended as an alternative to the long division demonstrated in class.

Decimal division

To make the division easier, multiply both numbers by as many 10's as needed to remove the decimal from the divisor. See the following examples.

$0.125\overline{)8}$ 3 decimal places so 10x10x10=x1000

$125.\overline{)8000.}$

$23.9\overline{)125.895}$ 1 decimal place in divisor so x10

$239.\overline{)1258.95}$

Once this is done carry on as done before using whatever method you are comfortable with.

Division as it was taught in class. There are some more decimal division samples as well.

$25\overline{)425}$	Start with the 1st leftmost number. Since $\frac{4}{25}$ is less than 1, include the next digit. Put an 'x' over the 4 as a place holder. $\frac{42}{25}$ this is bigger than 1, continue by subtracting 25 from 42
x10 $25\overline{)425}$ <u>**42**</u> **17**	$\frac{17}{25}$ is too small, add the next digit
x10 $25\overline{)425}$ <u>**42**</u> **175**	$\frac{175}{25}$ by trial and error, 25x8=200 too big 25x6 =150 25x7=175 exactly
x17 $25\overline{)425}$ <u>**42**</u> **175** <u>**175**</u> **0**	The '7' is added to the '10' already there. A quick check (25x17=425) proves this is right.

Here is another one.

24)390.	Try 1st digit only $\frac{\mathbf{3}}{\mathbf{24}}$ nope, try $\frac{\mathbf{39}}{\mathbf{24}}$, yep goes 1 time
***x*1 .** **24)390.** **<u>24</u>** **15**	Write the '1' up top, subtract the '24'. Try $\frac{\mathbf{15}}{\mathbf{24}}$ nope, bring down the next '0'
***x*1 .** **24)390.** **<u>24</u>** **150**	$\frac{\mathbf{150}}{\mathbf{24}}$ try 24x5=120, try 24x6=144 Close enough
***x*16.** **24)390.** **<u>24</u>** **150** **<u>144</u>**	Subtract, the answer 6 gives $\frac{\mathbf{6}}{\mathbf{24}}$ so bring down a zero
***x*16.** **24)390.** **<u>24</u>** **150** **<u>144</u>** **60**	$\frac{\mathbf{60}}{\mathbf{24}}$ goes evenly '2' times
***x*16.2** **24)390.** **<u>24</u>** **150** **<u>144</u>** **60** **<u>48</u>** **12**	Bring down another '0'
***x*16.2** **24)390.** **<u>24</u>** **150** **<u>144</u>** **60** **<u>48</u>** **120**	From just above, we know that 24x5=120.

x16.25 24) 390. 24 150 144 60 48 120 120 0	All done. A final check (24x16.25=390) so this is the right answer. Remember the 'x' is there only as a place holder. Final answer can be written as $\frac{390}{24} = 16.25$

The next pages will look at decimal division.

Decimal Division

$0.17\overline{)6.63}$	The divisor (0.17) should not have any decimal places. This is simply to make the division easier. Since 0.17 has two decimal places, multiply by as many '10's'. The number underneath the division sign is also multiplied by the '10's'.
$0.17\overline{)6.63}$ $x100\ x100$ $17\overline{)663.}$	Proceed the same as the examples on the previous pages. The answer is shown without the side notes.

$$\begin{array}{r} x39. \\ 17\overline{)663.} \\ \underline{51} \\ 153 \\ \underline{153} \\ 0 \end{array}$$

This is easily proved by multiplying 17x39 which gives 663.

$0.16\overline{)7.0776}$	Since there are 2 decimal places in 0.16, both numbers are multiplied by 100 (10x10).
$16\overline{)707.76}$	Problem proceeds as before.

$$\begin{array}{r} x44.235 \\ 16\overline{)707.76} \\ \underline{64} \\ 67 \\ \underline{64} \\ 3.7 \\ \underline{3.2} \\ .56 \\ \underline{.48} \\ 80 \\ \underline{80} \\ 0 \end{array}$$

Practice Questions – Multiplication and Division

Multiply the following

1. $145x24$
2. $326x178$
3. $4192x34$
4. $24x17$
5. $98x7$
6. $12.45x1.7$
7. $0.1234x78$
8. $78.0625x1.25$
9. $32.03125x0.125$
10. $64x0.0625$

Divide the following; some answers will have three decimal places.

1. $37\overline{)3552}$
2. $25\overline{)15300}$
3. $17\overline{)2516}$
4. $54\overline{)21168}$
5. $17\overline{)1207}$
6. $32\overline{)3976}$
7. $64\overline{)11424}$
8. $72\overline{)16902}$
9. $94\overline{)2291.25}$
10. $50\overline{)16081.25}$

Fractions

First there are some rules about fractions.

1. **$\frac{x}{x}$ is always "1" and x can be <u>ANYTHING</u>.**
2. **<u>Anything</u> x 1 = the same thing**

   $4 x 1 = 4$

   $y x 1 = y$

   $\frac{1}{4} x 1 = \frac{1}{4}$

Addition of Fractions

The bottom numbers in a fraction (the denominator) must be the same before addition (or subtraction) can take place.

Since multiplying by a value of 1 doesn't change the meaning, this is our goal.

$\frac{1}{2} + \frac{1}{3}$	**Chose the lowest number that both 2 and 3 can divide evenly into. "6"**
$\left(\frac{3}{3} x \frac{1}{2}\right) + \left(\frac{1}{3} x \frac{2}{2}\right)$	**Multiply each fraction by a unique value of 1. When multiplying it is top to top over bottom to bottom.**
$\left(\frac{3x1}{3x2}\right) + \left(\frac{1x2}{3x2}\right)$	**Finish this part**
$\frac{3}{6} + \frac{2}{6}$	**Add the top numbers only.**
$\frac{3+2}{6} = \frac{5}{6}$	**Finally, ask yourself if this is the smallest it can be and the answer is yes.**

$\frac{3}{4} - \frac{3}{16}$	**Chose the lowest number that both 4 and 16 can divide evenly into. "16"**
$\left(\frac{4}{4} x \frac{3}{4}\right) - \left(\frac{3}{16}\right)$	**Multiply the first fraction by a unique value of 1. When multiplying it is top to top over bottom to bottom.**
$\left(\frac{4x3}{4x4}\right) - \left(\frac{3}{16}\right)$	**Finish this part**
$\frac{12}{16} - \frac{3}{16}$	**Subtract the top numbers only.**
$\frac{12-3}{16} = \frac{9}{16}$	**Finally, ask yourself if this is the smallest it can be and the answer is yes.**

Reducing Fractions

Reducing fractions is actually the same process as getting a common denominator, just in reverse.

$\frac{2}{4}$	**Find the largest number that will divide evenly into each number. In this case the number would be "2"**
$\frac{2x1}{2x2} = \frac{2}{2} x \frac{1}{2}$	**Rewrite top and bottom as products of "2" and separate the fraction into 2 fractions as shown**
$1x\frac{1}{2} = \frac{1}{2}$	**Remember, anything divided by itself is a "1".**
$\frac{2}{4} = \frac{1}{2}$	**And that's it. If you picked the largest number, this should be the most reduced form of the original fraction. If not, repeat the process and reduce it again.** **With practice, this becomes faster.**

Here is another one.

$\frac{15}{40}$	**Find the largest number that will divide evenly into each number. In this case the number would be "5"**
$\frac{5x3}{5x8} = \frac{5}{5} x \frac{3}{8}$	**Rewrite top and bottom as products of "5" and separate the fraction into 2 fractions as shown**
$1x\frac{3}{8} = \frac{3}{8}$	**And that's it, you are done!**

Anytime fractions are added, subtracted, multiplied or divided, the answer should be checked to see if it can be reduced.

Improper Fractions

Improper fractions are simply fractions where the top number (numerator) is larger than the bottom number (denominator).

Example

$\frac{12}{8}$ would be called an improper fraction. Rewriting this as a mixed number (whole number and fraction) is similar to what you have done so far.

Several examples are shown on the next page. Study these carefully.

$$\frac{12}{8}=\frac{8+4}{8}=\frac{8}{8}+\frac{4}{8}=1+\frac{4}{8}=1\frac{4}{8}$$

Reduce the fraction.

1. $$\frac{4}{8}=\frac{4x1}{4x2}=\frac{4}{4}x\frac{1}{2}=\frac{1}{2}$$

   so $\frac{12}{8}=1\frac{1}{2}$

2. $$\frac{13}{4}=\frac{12+1}{4}=\frac{12}{4}+\frac{1}{4}=3+\frac{1}{4}=3\frac{1}{4}$$

3. $$\frac{54}{16}=\frac{48+6}{16}=\frac{48}{16}+\frac{6}{16}=3+\frac{6}{16}$$

   $$\frac{6}{16}=\frac{2x3}{2x8}=\frac{3}{8}$$

   so $\frac{54}{16}=3\frac{3}{8}$

Practice questions follow on the next page.

SHOP FRACTIONS PRACTICE SHEET

Solve the following and reduce if necessary.

1). $\frac{1}{2}+\frac{5}{4}$ 2). $\frac{3}{16}+\frac{13}{64}$ 3). $\frac{3}{2}+\frac{5}{8}$ 4). $\frac{1}{12}+\frac{3}{4}$

5). $\frac{1}{16}+\frac{17}{64}$ 6). $\frac{5}{4}+\frac{13}{32}$ 7). $\frac{5}{8}+\frac{13}{16}$ 8). $\frac{15}{16}+\frac{7}{64}$

9). $\frac{1}{32}+\frac{1}{16}$ 10). $\frac{7}{8}+\frac{13}{64}$ 11). $\frac{5}{4}+\frac{13}{16}$ 12). $\frac{17}{32}+\frac{39}{64}$

13). $\frac{1}{2}+\frac{3}{16}+\frac{5}{8}+\frac{11}{32}$

14). $\frac{5}{8}-\frac{1}{4}$ 15). $\frac{51}{64}-\frac{3}{16}$ 16). $\frac{5}{8}-\frac{3}{8}$ 17). $\frac{15}{16}-\frac{3}{4}$

18). $\frac{17}{64}-\frac{7}{32}$ 19). $\frac{15}{16}-\frac{3}{8}$ 20). $\frac{7}{8}-\frac{11}{32}$ 21). $\frac{17}{32}-\frac{7}{64}$

22). $\frac{35}{64}-\frac{1}{4}$ 23). $\frac{7}{8}-\frac{11}{64}$ 24). $\frac{7}{8}-\frac{13}{64}$ 25). $\frac{16}{32}-\frac{16}{64}$

26). $\frac{3}{4}-\frac{1}{8}-\frac{11}{64}$

Adding and Subtracting Mixed Numbers and Improper Fractions

Addition

Improper – change to a mixed number first and continue as shown in the table below.

$\frac{27}{8}+\frac{17}{4}$	**Change each of these to mixed numbers.**
$\left(\frac{24+3}{8}\right)+\left(\frac{16+1}{4}\right)$ $3+\frac{3}{8}+4+\frac{1}{4}$	**Rewrite the last line grouping whole numbers together and fractions separately. Remember fractions like these can be rewritten as follows:** $\frac{24+3}{8}=\frac{24}{8}+\frac{3}{8}$
$(3+4)+\left(\frac{3}{8}+\frac{1}{4}\right)$	**Add the whole numbers and find the common denominator for the fractions, in this case it will be "8".**
$7+\left(\frac{3}{8}+\frac{2}{8}\right)$	**Add the fractions, reduce if possible or if another improper was created, convert to a mixed number and continue.**
$7\frac{5}{8}$	**All done.**

If you didn't change the fractions to mixed numbers, you could add them as you would regular fractions, but the numerators would get very large.

Here are some more examples.

$$3\frac{1}{8}+2\frac{1}{4}$$

$$=(3+2)+\left(\frac{1}{8}+\frac{2}{8}\right)$$

$$=5\frac{3}{8}$$

$$\frac{13}{4}+\frac{5}{16}$$

$$=\frac{12+1}{4}+\frac{5}{16}=\frac{12}{4}+\frac{1}{4}+\frac{5}{16}$$

$$=3+\frac{1}{4}+\frac{5}{16}=3+\left(\frac{1}{4}x\frac{4}{4}\right)+\frac{5}{16}$$

$$=3+\frac{4}{16}+\frac{5}{16}$$

$$=3\frac{9}{16}$$

Watch what happens in this example.

$$3\frac{3}{4}+\frac{31}{16}$$
$$=3+\frac{3}{4}+1+\frac{15}{16}$$
$$=(3+1)+\frac{12}{16}+\frac{15}{16}$$
$$=4+\frac{27}{16}=4+\frac{16+11}{16}=4+\frac{16}{16}+\frac{11}{16}$$
$$=4+1+\frac{11}{16}$$
$$=5\frac{11}{16}$$

Since the fraction portion gave an improper fraction, it was broken down to a mixed number and then added to the whole number that was already there.

Subtraction

$2\frac{1}{4}-\frac{1}{3}$	**This starts the same as the addition did.**
$\left(2+\frac{1}{4}\right)-\left(\frac{1}{3}\right)$ $=2+\left(\frac{1}{4}-\frac{1}{3}\right)$	**Get a common denominator, in this case "12".**
$2+\left(\frac{3}{12}-\frac{4}{12}\right)$	**The first fraction is smaller and so we need to borrow.** **We will borrow a value of "1" from the whole number.**
$1+1+\frac{3}{12}-\frac{4}{12}$ $=1+\frac{12}{12}+\frac{3}{12}-\frac{4}{12}$	**Remember a number divided by itself is a 1. We chose 12 over 12 to have a common denominator with 3/12.** **Add all the fractions.**
$=1\frac{11}{12}$	**All done.**

The next page shows the same question done as improper fractions instead.

$$2\frac{1}{4}-\frac{1}{3}$$

$$=\frac{(2x4)+1}{4}-\frac{1}{3}$$

$$=\frac{9}{4}-\frac{1}{3}$$

=

$$=\left(\frac{3}{3}x\frac{9}{4}\right)-\left(\frac{1}{3}x\frac{4}{4}\right)$$

$$=\frac{27}{12}-\frac{4}{12}=\frac{23}{12}=\frac{12+11}{12}$$

$$=1\frac{11}{12}$$

Here are some more subtraction examples.

1.

$$3\frac{1}{2}-1\frac{1}{4}$$

$$(3-1)+\left(\frac{1}{2}-\frac{1}{4}\right)$$

$$=2+\left(\frac{2}{4}-\frac{1}{4}\right)$$ no need to borrow, so carry on...

$$=2\frac{1}{4}$$

2.

$$8\frac{1}{16}-3\frac{1}{4}$$

$$=(8-3)+\left(\frac{1}{16}-\frac{1}{4}\right)$$

$$=5+\left(\frac{1}{16}-\frac{4}{16}\right)$$ this will need a borrow...

$$=4+\frac{16}{16}+\frac{1}{16}-\frac{4}{16}$$

$$=4\frac{13}{16}$$

Multiplication and Division of fractions

Multiplication

This is the easiest of all. See below for some examples.

1. $\frac{3}{4} x \frac{3}{8} = \frac{3x3}{4x8}$

$= \frac{9}{32}$

2. $\frac{10}{4} x \frac{3}{8} = \frac{10x3}{4x8} = \frac{30}{32} = \frac{15}{16}$

Alternate method - reduce if possible and continue

$\frac{10}{4} x \frac{3}{8} = \frac{\cancel{2}x5}{\cancel{2}x2} x \frac{3}{8} = \frac{5x3}{2x8} = \frac{15}{16}$

3. $3\frac{1}{4} x 2\frac{1}{8}$

$= \frac{(3x4)+1}{4} x \frac{(2x8)+1}{8}$

$= \frac{13}{4} x \frac{17}{8}$

$= \frac{221}{32} = \frac{192+29}{32} = 6\frac{29}{32}$

Division

The rule here is to flip over the second (2nd) fraction and multiply.

Samples

$1 \div \frac{1}{2}$

$= 1x \frac{2}{1}$

$= 2$

$\frac{1}{4} \div \frac{1}{8}$

$= \frac{1}{4} x \frac{8}{1} = \frac{8}{4}$

$= 2$

$3\frac{1}{4} \div 2\frac{1}{8}$ improper fractions first

$\frac{(3x4)+1}{4} \div \frac{(2x8)+1}{8}$

$= \frac{13}{4} \div \frac{17}{8}$ continue as before now

$= \frac{13}{4} x \frac{8}{17}$

$= \frac{13x8}{4x17} = \frac{8x13}{4x17} = \frac{\cancel{4}x2x13}{\cancel{4}x17}$

$= \frac{26}{17} = \frac{17+9}{17} = \frac{17}{17} + \frac{9}{17}$

$= 1\frac{9}{17}$

Practice questions follow.

Solve the following and reduce if necessary.

1). $\frac{1}{2} x \frac{5}{8}$ 2). $\frac{3}{4} x \frac{13}{64}$ 3). $\frac{3}{8} x \frac{5}{8}$ 4). $\frac{1}{2} x \frac{3}{4}$

5). $\frac{1}{32} x \frac{17}{64}$ 6). $\frac{5}{8} x \frac{13}{16}$ 7). $\frac{5}{8} x \frac{13}{32}$ 8). $\frac{15}{32} x \frac{7}{64}$

9). $\frac{1}{32} x \frac{1}{8}$ 10). $\frac{7}{8} x \frac{13}{32}$ 11). $\frac{5}{8} x \frac{13}{64}$ 12). $\frac{17}{32} x \frac{39}{64}$

13). $\left(\frac{1}{2} x \frac{3}{4}\right) x \frac{5}{8}$

14). $\frac{5}{8} \div \frac{1}{2}$ 15). $\frac{51}{64} \div \frac{3}{4}$ 16). $\frac{5}{8} \div \frac{3}{8}$ 17). $\frac{7}{8} \div \frac{3}{4}$

18). $\frac{17}{64} \div \frac{1}{32}$ 19). $\frac{13}{16} \div \frac{5}{8}$ 20). $\frac{5}{8} \div \frac{13}{32}$ 21). $\frac{15}{32} \div \frac{7}{64}$

22). $\frac{1}{2} \div \frac{35}{64}$ 23). $\frac{7}{8} \div \frac{13}{32}$ 24). $\frac{5}{8} \div \frac{13}{64}$ 25). $\frac{29}{32} \div \frac{39}{64}$

26). $\left(\frac{3}{4} \div \frac{1}{2}\right) \div \frac{11}{64}$

Fractions to Decimals Conversion

To convert a fraction to a decimal, simply divide the top by the bottom.

$$\frac{1}{2} = 2\overline{)1.0}^{\;0.5} \quad \frac{1}{2} = 0.5$$

$$\frac{3}{4} = 4\overline{)3.00}^{\;0.75} \quad \frac{3}{4} = 0.75$$

With improper fractions, first convert it to a mixed number and then change the fraction to a decimal and add it to the whole number.

$$\frac{13}{4} = 3\frac{1}{4}$$

$$4\overline{)1.00}^{\;0.25} \qquad 3 + 0.25 = 3.25$$

$$\text{so } \frac{13}{4} = 3.25$$

In the example above, if you actually divided the 13 by the 4 you will also get 3.25 as an answer. The way demonstrated in the example is better if you are doing these without a calculator.

Decimals to Fractions

Common shop fractions and their decimal equivalents

$\frac{1}{2}$	**0.5**
$\frac{1}{4}$	**0.25**
$\frac{1}{8}$	**0.125**
$\frac{1}{16}$	**0.0625**
$\frac{1}{32}$	**0.03125**
$\frac{1}{64}$	**0.015625**

Knowing these is handy if you have to convert a shop fraction into a decimal value and you don't have a calculator nearby.

Example

$$\frac{3}{8} = 3x\frac{1}{8} = 3x0.125 = 0.375$$

$$\frac{15}{64} = 15x\frac{1}{64} = 15x0.015625 = 0.234375$$

To convert any decimal to the nearest shop fraction, see the following examples.

0.285714285 as 32^{nds}

$0.285714285x32 = 9.142857143$ round to the nearest whole number

$$0.285714285 \cong \frac{9}{32}$$

$\frac{24}{7}$ to the nearest $\frac{1}{8}th$

$$\frac{24}{7} = 3.42857142857 = 3 + 0.42857142857$$

$$0.42857142857x8 = 3$$

so $\frac{24}{7} \cong 3\frac{3}{8}$

Practice Questions follow

Fractions to Decimals Practice Questions

Convert the following to their decimal equivalent

1. $\frac{1}{4} =$
2. $\frac{1}{2} =$
3. $\frac{3}{4} =$
4. $\frac{5}{16} =$
5. $\frac{7}{8} =$
6. $1\frac{1}{8} =$
7. $2\frac{1}{4} =$
8. $3\frac{1}{32} =$
9. $7\frac{1}{8} =$
10. $12\frac{7}{64} =$

Decimals to Fractions Practice Questions

Sample

$0.46875 =$ __________

Rewrite as a fraction over 1 and as many zeros as decimal places

$\frac{46875}{100000}$ Reduce this

Since the top number ends in a '5' we can expect 5, 25, 125 to work.

Let's start with '125'

$\frac{\cancel{125} x 375}{\cancel{125} x 800}$ Reduce again, this time let's try 25

$\frac{\cancel{25} x 15}{\cancel{25} x 32}$ This can not be reduced any further so...

$0.46875 = \frac{15}{32}$

Questions

1. 0.1875 =
2. 0.375 =
3. 0.34375 =
4. 0.4375 =
5. 0.125 =
6. 2.25 =
7. 11.125 =
8. 24.375 =
9. 9.4375 =
10. 17.625 =

Percents

Percents fall into a special application of fractions and decimals and literally means 'per 100'.

So $27\% = \frac{27}{100} = 0.27$ **Any of the three forms is appropriate and depends on the application.**

Basic percentage problems fall into one of three types and all deal with only three quantities; the *base*, which is the value we are taking the percent of; the rate or *percent* value; and the *amount* or answer that we get when we multiply the base by the rate. In equation form this becomes $A = PB$ **where the rate P is written as its decimal equivalent.**

Type 1 Problem Finding the Amount when Base and rate (P) are known

What is 35% of 80.0?

$35\% = 0.35$

Since the value '80.0' follows the phrase ' percent of' it is the base value.

$\therefore \mathbf{A} = \mathbf{PB}$

$\therefore \mathbf{A} = (0.35)80.0 = 28.0$

Type 2 Problem Finding the Base when a Rate is known

12% of what number is 78?

$$\mathbf{B} = \frac{\mathbf{A}}{\mathbf{P}}$$

replace phrase 'of what number' with x

$12\%\mathbf{x} = 78$

$0.12\mathbf{x} = 78$

$$\mathbf{x} = \frac{78}{0.12} = 650$$

Type 3 Problem Finding the Rate when the Amount and Base are known

42.0 is what percent of 405?

$$P = \frac{A}{B}$$

$$P = \frac{42.0}{405} = 0.103703703 = 10.4\%$$

Tolerances

In a trades application, tolerances (or clearances) are calculated to control how well pieces of a job will fit together.

ex. $120mm \pm 15\%$ **This means that the actual length is between 138mm and 102mm.**

$\text{max value} = 120\text{x}0.15 = 18\text{mm}, \quad \text{total} = 120 + 18 = 138\text{mm}$

$\text{min value} = 120\text{x}0.15 = 18\text{mm}, \quad \text{total} = 120 - 18 = 102\text{mm}$

When the $\pm$ is used, it is looking for both the maximum and minimum value. This is known as a *bilateral tolerance*. A *unilateral tolerance* looks only for the maximum or the minimum.

$25 + 0.1\%$

$25 + (25x0.001) = 25 + 0.025 = \underline{\underline{25.025}}$

or

$25 - 0.1\%$

$25 - (25x0.001) = 25 - 0.025 = \underline{\underline{24.975}}$

Tolerances for increased accuracy can be also be expressed as measurement changes rather than percentages.

$2.132 \pm 0.005 = \underline{\underline{2.137 \text{ to } 2.127}}$

The following are tolerances that are used to describe the degree of fit between two parts.

Minimum Clearance – is the smallest allowable gap between two interlocking parts.

Maximum interference – is the largest allowable overlap between two parts (commonly seen in a press fit).

Minimum Interference – is the smallest allowable overlap between two parts (commonly seen in a press fit).

Mean dimension – is the average dimension between the maximum and minimum values.

1. $2.132 \pm 0.005 = 2.137$ to 2.127

   The mean dimension will be $\frac{2.137 + 2.127}{2} = \underline{\underline{2.132}}$

2. $1.475^{+0.005}_{-0.004} = 1.48$ to 1.471

   The mean dimension will be $\frac{1.48 + 1.471}{2} = \underline{\underline{1.4755}}$

Tolerance Sample Problems

Fill in the Table

	Tolerance	Maximum Value	Minimum Value
1.		$5\frac{7}{16}$	$5\frac{13}{32}$
2.	**0.03″**	**16.76″**	
3.	**0.007″**		**0.904″**

Solutions:

1. **Find the change and divide by 2**

$$= 5\frac{7}{16} - 5\frac{13}{32}$$

$$= 5\frac{14}{32} - 5\frac{13}{32} = \frac{1}{32}$$

$$\frac{1}{32} \div 2 = \frac{1}{32} x \frac{1}{2} = \underline{\frac{1}{64}}$$

$$\text{Tolerance} = \pm\frac{1}{64}$$

2. **Double the tolerance and subtract from maximum value**

$$Max - (2xTol) = Min$$

$$16.76 - (2x0.03) = 16.76 - 0.06 = \underline{16.70}$$

Minimum Value is 16.7"

3. **Double the tolerance and add it to the minimum value**

$$Min + (2xTol) = Max$$

$$0.904 + (2x0.007) = 0.904 + 0.014 = \underline{0.918}$$

Maximum Value is 0.918"

Fill in the Table

	Maximum Value	Mean	Minimum Value	Tolerance
1.	42.125		41.875	
2.	187.625	187.25		
3.	21.001			+0.003 -0.000

Solutions

1.

$$\text{Mean} = \frac{\text{Max + Min}}{2}$$

$$Mean = \frac{42.125 + 41.875}{2} = \frac{84}{2} = \underline{42}$$

To find the tolerances, now compare the max and min values to the mean.

$$Max - Mean = 42.125 - 42 = 0.125$$
$$Mean - Min = 42 - 41.875 = 0.125$$
$$Tolerance = \underline{\pm 0.125}$$

2.

$$Max - Mean = Tol$$
$$187.625 - 187.25 = 0.375$$
$$Min = 187.25 - 0.375 = \underline{186.875}$$
$$Tolerances = \underline{\pm 0.375}$$

3.

$$Mean = Max - Tol$$
$$Mean = 21.001 - 0.003 = \underline{20.998}$$
$$Min = Mean - 0.000 = \underline{20.998}$$

Percentages Practice Sheet

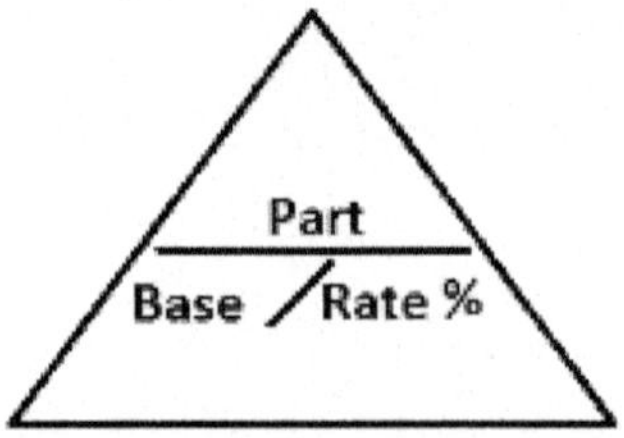

$$Rate\% = \frac{Part}{Base}$$

$$Part = Base \times Rate\%$$

$$Base = \frac{Part}{Rate\%}$$

TYPE 1 Finding Part when Rate and Base is Given

1. 40% of 60.15
2. 70% of 198.86
3. 29% of 169.12
4. 72% of 816.7
5. 115% of 53.8
6. 232% of 1.18
7. 6.5% of 59.65
8. $8\frac{1}{4}$% of 283.41
9. $7\frac{1}{8}$% of 3025.63
10. 9.04% of 12476.09

TYPE 2 Finding the Base (Whole) when the Part and Rate is Given

Round answers to two (2) decimal places

	Part	Base(Whole)	Rate %
1.	16		2
2.	12		25
3.	40		17.5
4.	8.125		16 ¼
5.	354		59
6.	16.56		23
7.	31.5		35
8.	72		12
9.	418.95		57
10.	336.2		41

Continued on the next page

TYPE 3 Finding Rate when Part and Base is Given

Complete the table accurate to one decimal place.

	Part	Base(Whole)	Percent
1.	4	16	
2.	10	25	
3.	27	60	
4.	11.6	16	
5.	9	27	
6.	18	270	
7.	63	64	
8.	15	32	
9.	12	64	
10.	2.5	200	

Tolerances

Fill in the Table

Question	Tolerance	Maximum Value	Minimum Value
1.	$\frac{1}{8}$"	$25\frac{7}{32}$"	
2.		12.40625″	12.34375″
3.	0.006″		2.806″
4.	0.007mm	289.012mm	
5.		62.14mm	61.94mm

Fill in the Table

Question	Maximum Value	Mean	Minimum Value	Tolerance
1.			$27\frac{31}{32}$	$\pm\frac{1}{32}$
2.		17.504		$\pm$0.0475
3.	$2\frac{15}{16}$	$2\frac{7}{8}$		
4.	21.4375		20.6875	
5.		285		$\pm$0.0625

Signed Numbers

Addition

– if all numbers are positive, then the answer is positive

- **If the numbers are both positive and negative, rewrite the statement using brackets, simplify the brackets and add the results.**

Sample

$2-3+4-1+5-7+10-6=$

$(2+4+5+10)+(-3-1-7-6)=$

$21+(-17)=$

4

Subtraction

– if the signs BETWEEN the numbers are different, the answer is negative; if the signs BETWEEN the numbers are the same then the answer is positive.

Sample

1) $-4+^{-}7=-4-7=\underline{-11}$
2) $4-^{+}7=4-7=\underline{-3}$
3) $4-^{-}8=4+8=\underline{12}$
4) $4+^{+}5=\underline{9}$

Multiplication/Division

– if the signs are the same the answer is positive; if the signs are different the answer is negative.

Sample

1) $\frac{-12}{-3}=\underline{4}$
2) $-12x-3=\underline{36}$
3) $12x-3=-12x3=\underline{-36}$
4) $\frac{-36}{12}=\frac{36}{-12}=\underline{-3}$

<u>Square and Cube Roots</u> – Since every application deals with a measurement that is always a positive number, all answers are positive. There will be more on this in the Powers and Roots section.

Practice work follows on the next page.

Signed Numbers Practice Questions

1) $-3+7=$ ______ 2) $-2-8=$ ______

3) $-3+^{-}7=$ ______ 4) $2-^{-}8=$ ______

5) $-7-^{-}28=$ ______ 6) $-32-18=$ ______

7) $-3x7=$ ______ 8) $-2\div 8=$ ______

9) $-3x^{-}7=$ ______ 10) $-32\div^{-}8=$ ______

11) $-21\div 3=$ ______ 12) $48\div^{-}16=$ ______

Angles – Decimal Degrees (DD) and Degrees Minutes Seconds (DMS)

Decimal degrees are what normally appear on the calculator after doing a trig (sin, cos, tan) function. DMS is used for more accuracy.

In DMS 1 degree is like 1 hour. An hour can be broken up into 60 minutes and each minute can be broken up into 60 seconds.

$$\mathbf{1^\circ = 1\ hour = 60'}$$
$$\mathbf{1' = 60''}$$
$$\mathbf{00^\circ 00' 00''}\ \ \textbf{standard form DMS}$$

To convert from DD to DMS (long way)

Example 1:

$\mathbf{27.149857^\circ}$	$\mathbf{27^\circ}$
$\mathbf{0.149857^\circ x 60 = 8.99142}$	$\mathbf{8'}$
$\mathbf{0.99142 x 60 = 59.4852}$	$\mathbf{59''}$

$$\mathbf{27.149857^\circ = 27^\circ 8' 59''}$$

Example 2:

$\mathbf{57.4925^\circ}$	$\mathbf{57^\circ}$
$\mathbf{0.4925^\circ x 60 = 29.55'}$	$\mathbf{29'}$
$\mathbf{0.55 x 60 = 33''}$	$\mathbf{33''}$

$$\mathbf{57.4925^\circ = 57^\circ 29' 33''}$$

To convert from DMS to DD

Example 1:

$$\mathbf{45^\circ 14' 37''}$$
$$= \mathbf{45^\circ} + \left(\frac{\mathbf{14'}}{\mathbf{60'}}\right) + \left(\frac{\mathbf{37''}}{\mathbf{3600''}}\right)$$
$$= \mathbf{45.24361111^\circ} = \underline{\mathbf{45.2436^\circ}}$$

Example 2:

$$\mathbf{57^\circ 29' 33''}$$
$$= \mathbf{57^\circ} + \left(\frac{\mathbf{29'}}{\mathbf{60'}}\right) + \left(\frac{\mathbf{33''}}{\mathbf{3600''}}\right)$$
$$= \underline{\mathbf{57.4925^\circ}}$$

Adding DMS angles

The only thing to keep in mind is that 60″=1′ and that 1′ = 1°.

Example 1:

45°37'42"
+ 23°41'28"
68°~~78~~'~~70~~"
1' 10" → this was 70"
1°18' → this was 78'
69°19'10"

Example 2:

78°19'58"
+ 64°23 22"
142°42'~~80~~"
1' 20" → this was 80"
142°43'20"

Subtracting DMS Angles

To subtract DMS angles, borrowing means changing 1° to 60′, or 1′ to 60″ and adding it to the value before you subtract.

78°19'58"
− 64°23'22" Since 19′ is less than 23′ I'll borrow 1° and add 60′ to 19′

7~~8~~ 7°79'58"
− 64° 23'22" This can be checked easily with a calculator that has DMS and DD functions.
13° 56' 36"

Degrees, DMS and operations

Practice Questions.

Convert to DMS

	DD	DMS
1	27.3475°	
2	33.7894°	
3	45.01345°	
4	78.71492°	
5	12.112985°	
6	22.63459°	
7	10.985432°	
8	17.56473°	
9	25.375°	
10	61.0375°	

Convert to DD

	DMS	DD
1	48°21'09"	
2	24°16'58"	
3	71°33'12"	
4	43°15'15"	
5	12°55'48"	
6	32°19'01"	
7	51°31'44"	
8	13°45'56"	
9	77°38'11"	
10	53°27'45"	

Add the following

1. 45°16'54" + 17°43'17"

2. 115°23'41" + 62°15'23"

3. 63°22'01" + 21°16'25"

4. 56°20'32" + 21°34'18"

5. 71°42'21" + 33°51'34"

Subtract the following

1. $\begin{array}{r} 45^\circ16'54'' \\ -17^\circ43'17'' \\ \hline \end{array}$

2. $\begin{array}{r} 115^\circ23'41'' \\ -\ 62^\circ15'23'' \\ \hline \end{array}$

3. $\begin{array}{r} 63^\circ22'01'' \\ -21^\circ16'25'' \\ \hline \end{array}$

4. $\begin{array}{r} 56^\circ20'32'' \\ -21^\circ34'18'' \\ \hline \end{array}$

5. $\begin{array}{r} 71^\circ42'21'' \\ -33^\circ51'34'' \\ \hline \end{array}$

Order of Operations

There are two versions of this. This section will explain and demonstrate the most complete version, the BEDMAS system.

BEDMAS stands for:

Letter	Explanation
B	**Brackets. This are done first from left to right and there are nested sets, the innermost is where you begin and then work your way out. See the sample.**
E	**Exponents (or powers) if they are present**
D	**Division**
M	**Multiplication**
A	**Addition**
S	**Subtraction**

Sample 1

$\left(\left(\left(\underline{(4-7)}x-2\right)+8\right)\div 2\right)$ Start here

$\left(\left(\underline{(-3)(x-2)}+8\right)\div 2\right)$ do next

$\left(\underline{(6+8)}\div 2\right)$ do next

$(14\div 2)$

$=7$

While this may have been an extreme example, it still demonstrates the idea of nested sets of brackets.

Sample 2

$4+7x2-3\div 4$ there are no brackets here so insert your own around the x and $\div$

$4+(7x2)-(3\div 4)$

$4+14-\dfrac{3}{4}$

$=17\dfrac{1}{4}=17.25$

Exercises follow...

Order of Operations Questions

1) $89-2x2=$ ______
2) $6+2x6=$ ______
3) $2x9+7=$ ______
4) $73-2x8=$ ______
5) $6^2+3x4-2=$ ______
6) $27-3^3=$ ______
7) $5^2+1^2=$ ______
8) $5+4^2-10\div 2=$ ______
9) $(3+8)x(4-9)=$ ______
10) $(49-(2+8))x2=$ ______

Powers and Roots

Powers

There are times when a number needs to be multiplied by itself more than once. For example, if we needed the volume of a cube that measured 8 inches per side the volume would be calculated as:

$V = l \times w \times h$

$= 8x8x8$

$= 512$ cubic inches

There is a convenient way to abbreviate both the multiplication and the units. The use of a power on the number or the unit shows us how many times it is multiplied by itself. The same volume problem then can be rewritten as:

$V = l \times w \times h$

$= 8^3$

$= 512\ in^3$

Here are some more examples of how a multiplication can be shortened (simplified)

$2x2 = 2^2$

$3x3x3 = 3^3$

$5x5x5x5 = 5^4$

foot x foot x foot $= ft^3$

The number (or word) is known as *the base* and the small number written above it (called a superscript) is known as *the power*.

$base^{power}$

A power of zero, regardless what the base is ALWAYS is equal to 1.

Roots

A root is the opposite of a power. So if $x^2 = y$ then $x = \sqrt{y}$**.**

if $3^2 = 9$ then $\sqrt{9} = 3$

Since all your applications deal with positive numbers, all answers are positives. The simplest explanation is that a length isn't thought of as a negative number.

The √ symbol, which can also look like this $\sqrt{\ }$ **is known as a square root. It asks the question 'What number multiplied by itself will give the number under the root sign**

Here are some common squares and their roots.

$2^2 = 4 \quad \sqrt{4} = 2$

$3^2 = 9 \quad \sqrt{9} = 3$

$4^2 = 16 \quad \sqrt{16} = 4$

$5^2 = 25 \quad \sqrt{25} = 5$

Cubes and Cube roots

If a cube power (3) means to multiply a number by itself 3 times, then a cube root asks what number multiplied by itself 3 times will give the number under the root sign.

$3 \times 3 \times 3 = 3^3 = 27 \qquad \sqrt[3]{27} = 3$

Notice that to tell the difference between a square root and a cube root, the number of the root sits in the notch of the root sign. Square and cube roots however will be the most common application for you.

All scientific calculators will have a x^y button. Most will have a square root and a cube root button as well. Check with your owner's manual or teacher on how to use the button correctly.

Powers and Roots Practice questions

1) 4^3 = ______	2) 2^2 = ______
3) 1^3 = ______	4) 8^2 = ______
5) 2.5^3 = ______	6) $\sqrt{100}$ = ______
7) $\sqrt[3]{64}$ = ______	8) $\sqrt{121}$ = ______
9) $\sqrt[3]{1000}$ = ______	10) $\sqrt{256}$ = ______

Ratios and Indirect Proportions

Ratios/Direct Proportions

A ratio is simply another way to express a fraction and it happens to be the most commonly used form in a real life application. Because the ratio is the same as a fraction, all the rules for fractions can be used here as well.

For example, in roofing a 7/12 (or 7:12) roof pitch means a 7" height change for every 12" length.

Sample: If a house is 40' wide with a 7/12 pitch, what is the height at the peak of the roof?

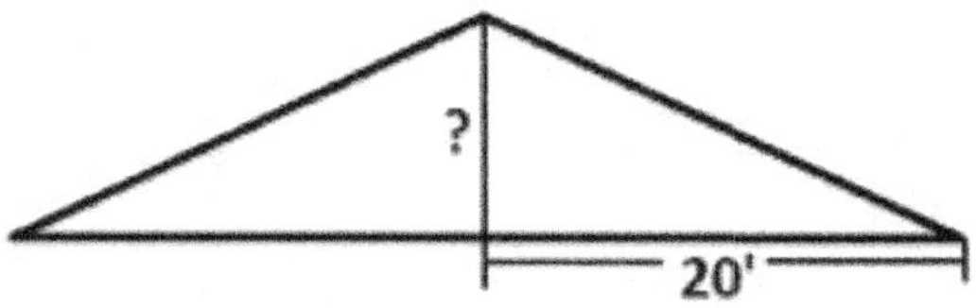

$$\frac{7}{12} = \frac{h}{240"}$$

$$h = \frac{7x240"}{12"} = 140" = 11'8" = 11.75'$$

Another example would be if Motor A is running at 3 times the speed of Motor B, what is the ratio?

Solution

$$\frac{MotorA}{MotorB} = \frac{3}{1}$$

In the case of automobile real axle ratios, we say that "the axle has a 3.27 ratio."

This means a ratio of 3.27:1 or $\frac{3.27}{1}$

The roof pitch example and the ones after it are known as 'direct ratios' or 'direct proportions'. This is also true in scale measurements on blueprints and maps.

For example, 1" is 25 miles on the map scale, so how far away is $2\frac{13}{16}$**"?**

Solution

Set up the ratios and solve as follows:

$$\frac{1''}{25 \text{ miles}} = \frac{2\frac{13}{16}''}{y \text{ miles}}$$

$$\frac{1}{25} = \frac{2.8125}{y} \quad \text{cross multiply}$$

$$y = 25x2.8125 = \underline{\underline{70.3125 \text{ miles}}}$$

This next example can also be used to demonstrate what a proportion is. A proportion is simply two equal ratios expressed as a ratio statement.

$7:12::x:240$ is the same as writing

$7:12 = x:240$ is the same as writing

$\frac{7}{12} = \frac{x}{240}$ Note that the :: means the same thing as the = sign

As you can see a proportion is another way to describe equal ratios.

Indirect Proportions

With the indirect proportions, the trick here is that as one value increases the other value decreases. For example, as we heat air its volume increases (direct) but its density decreases (indirect). Hot air balloons rely on this principle in order to fly.

Pulleys and gears also behave in this way. A gear or pulley with a small diameter wi[ll] have higher rpms than a gear or pulley with a large diameter.

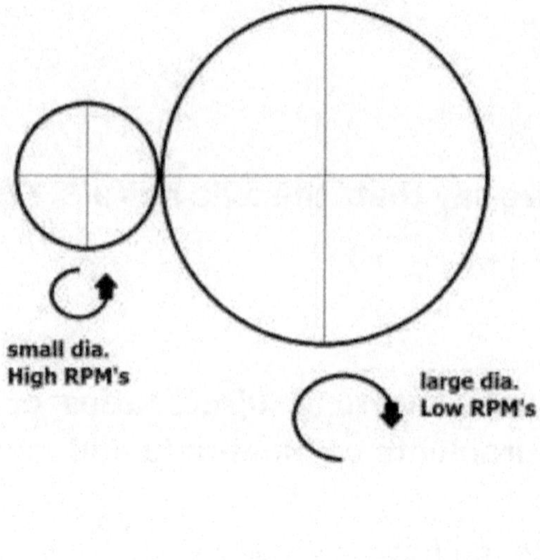

To set up a solution for an indirect proportion, write the SECOND ratio opposite to the FIRST ratio. See the following example.

An electric motor running at 1750 rpm is connected to a 5" diameter pulley. What pulley is required on the driven shaft to turn at 875 rpm?

Solution

Motor: driven shaft:: shaft pulley: motor pulley

$$\frac{\text{Motor}}{\text{Driven}} = \frac{\text{Driven Pulley}}{\text{Motor Pulley}}$$

$$\frac{1750}{875} = \frac{y}{5} \quad \text{cross multiply}$$

$$875y = 5x1750$$

$$875y = 8750$$

$$y = \underline{\underline{10"}}$$

Here is another one.

The volume of a gas is inversely proportional to the pressure upon it. (As pressure increases, volume decreases)

If the volume of a gas is 740 cu ft. at 16 psi, what is the volume if pressure is increased to 30 psi?

Solution

$$\frac{740ft^3}{y\ ft^3} = \frac{30}{16}$$

$$30y = 16x740$$

$$30y = 11840$$

$$y = \underline{\underline{394.67\ ft^3}}$$

If we were to use letters to represent the idea of an inverse proportion it would look like this:

$\frac{A_1}{B_1} = \frac{B_2}{A_2}$ **where the second ratio is the inverse (upside down) version of the first.**

Practice Questions

Direct Ratios/Proportions

Solve for 'x'.

1. $\frac{27}{40}=\frac{x}{100}$

2. $\frac{12}{x}=\frac{8}{50}$

3. $\frac{x}{7}=\frac{9}{21}$

4. $\frac{x}{5}=\frac{27}{45}$

5. $\frac{2\frac{1}{2}}{3\frac{1}{2}}=\frac{x}{14}$

Practical Questions

6. **8′ of steel beam (W16x57) is used. How much does 6′ weigh?**

7. **12′ of steel beam (W16x50) is used in a girder build. The build will require 125 beams to be delivered. What is the total weight of the delivery?**

8. **A beam that is 3.66 m (W410x46) is used. How much will 2.93 m weigh?**

9. **A machinist creates 1.25 kg of shavings from fabricating 16 rods. How many kg will be produced from fabricating 120 rods?**

10. **A welder can make 10 4″ welds in 40 minutes. How many welds can be done in 4 hours?**

Indirect Ratios/Proportions

These practice questions can be set up using one of the proportions below.

Read each question carefully.

Gears $\frac{\text{rpm Gear A}}{\text{rpm Gear B}} = \frac{\text{\# teeth Gear B}}{\text{\# teeth Gear A}}$

Pulleys $\frac{\text{rpm A}}{\text{rpm B}} = \frac{\text{Dia B}}{\text{Dia A}}$

Gases $\frac{\text{pressure } P_1}{\text{pressure } P_2} = \frac{\text{volume } V_2}{\text{volume } V_1}$

Questions

1. **A pair of belted pulleys have diameters of 21″ and 18″ respectively. If the larger spins at 2000 rpm, what does the smaller gear spin at?**

2. **A gear with 36 teeth makes 8 ½ revolutions per minute (rpm). What is the rpm of a gear with 22 teeth that is being turned by the larger gear?**

3. **Nitrogen is compressed from a volume of 300 ml down to a volume of 0.36 ml. At this smaller volume, pressure is measured to be 400 Pa. What pressure was the original volume at?**

4. **A sample of gas that occupies 600 ml under 90 kPa has the pressure increased to 150 kPa. What is the new volume of the gas?**

5. **A gas occupies 525 ml at 104.66 kPa. What is the volume when the pressure is reduced to 99.33 kPa?**

6. **A gas occupies 478 cm^3 at 104.1 kPa. What is the volume when the pressure is reduced to 88.2 kPa?**

7. **Initial volume is 75 ml at 145 atm of pressure. What is the pressure when the volume is 500 ml?**

8. **A motor is spinning at 800 rpm. This spins a gear with a diameter of 2 ¼″. What is the diameter of the gear required to reduce this to an rpm of 125?**

9. A pair of belted pulleys have respective diameters of 16" and 13 ½". If the smaller spins at 2000 rpm, what is the rpm of the larger pulley?

10. Two connected gears are spinning at 500 and 1250 rpm's. If the higher speed gear has a diameter of 10 cm, what is the diameter of the lower rpm gear?

Metric System Notes

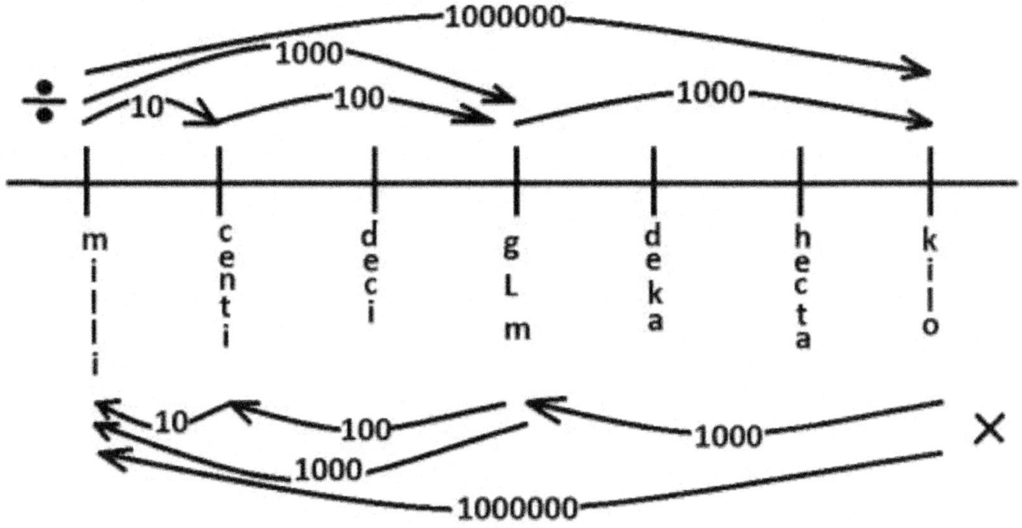

Common Metric Unit Conversions

The table above shows the conversions between the most commonly used values of the metric system.

The simplest list that the metals trades will deal with are the units of milli, centi and kilo with either the gram (g), liter (L) or meter (m) units.

Here is the simple list with its conversions.

Units you have	Units you want	Do this
milli	centi	÷10
centi	milli	x10
milli	meter	÷1000
meter	milli	x1000
centi	meter	÷100
meter	centi	x100
Kilo	meter	x1000
meter	kilo	÷1000

This conversion works whether you are dealing with millimeters (mm), millilitres (mL) or milligrams (mg). This is why the metric system was adopted by most of the world.

Standard (Old English) System

In this system we find the older measurement terms like: feet, inches, pounds, ounces, quarts, gallons and such. There are also a collection of older values like grains, bushels, drams etc.

With so many names for essentially the same thing, it was practical to change to a system where one value exists per usage. See the table below for examples of this.

Length Units	
Standard	**Metric**
Inch **Foot** **Yard** **Mile** **hand**	**Meter**
Volume Units	
Standard	**Metric**
Ounce **Cup** **Pint** **Quart** **gallon**	**Litre**
Mass Units	
Standard	**Metric**
Ounce **Pound** **Stone** **carat**	**Gram**

It is obviously easier to work in the metric system. Both systems however are still in use. Use the conversion table on the next page to convert the most commonly used values.

Linear To go from	into	Divide by	To go from	into	Multiply by
Centimeter (cm)	Inch (in)	2.54	Meter (m)	Inch (in)	39.37
Millimeter (mm)	Feet (ft)	304.8	Meter (m)	Feet (ft)	3.2808
Millimeter (mm)	Inch (in)	25.4	Meter (m)	Yard (yd)	1.0936
Inch (in)	Meter (m)	39.37	Inch (in)	Centimeter (cm)	2.54
Feet (ft)	Meter (m)	3.281	Inch (in)	Millimeter (mm)	25.4
Yard (yd)	Meter (m)	1.0936	Feet (ft)	Centimeter (cm)	30.48
AREA To go from	Into	Divide by	To go from	into	Multiply by
Square foot (ft^2)	Square Meter (m^2)	10.764	Square inch (in^2)	Square centimeter (cm^2)	6.4516
Square centimeter (cm^2)	Square inch (in^2)	6.4516	Square meter (m^2)	Square foot (ft^2)	10.7639
Square millimeter (mm^2)	Square inch (in^2)	645.16	Square inch (in^2)	Square millimeter (mm^2)	645.16
Volume To go from	Into	Divide by	To go from	into	Multiply by
Cubic centimeter (cm^3)	Cubic inch (in^3)	16.387	Cubic inch (in^3)	Cubic centimeter (cm^3)	16.387
Cubic feet (ft^3)	Cubic meter (m^3)	35.31	Cubic meter (m^3)	Cubic feet (ft^3)	35.31
Cubic millimeter (mm^3)	Cubic inch (in^3)	16,387.1	Cubic inch (in^3)	Cubic millimeter (mm^3)	16,387.1

Liquid Volume Conversions

To go From	to	Multiply by	To go From	To	Divide By
yd^3	m^3	0.76455	m^3	yd^3	0.76455
m^3	gal(UK)	219.969	gal(UK)	m^3	219.969
m^3	gal(US)	264.172	gal(US)	m^3	264.172
m^3	ft^3	35.3147	ft^3	m^3	35.3147
L	gal(UK)	0.219969	gal(UK)		0.219969
L	gal(US)	0.264172	gal(US)		0.264172

Conversions Practice

1. **0.375 mi = x yd**
2. **0.375 mi = x ft**
3. **6.541 km = x m**
4. **8.689 kg = x g**
5. **7.75 mi = x ft**
6. **1.375 mi = x yd**
7. **0.605 km = x m**
8. **93 in = x ft**
9. **62 in = x ft**
10. **14 cm = x mm**
11. **6.015 km = x m**
12. **203 cm = x m**
13. **2.417 ft = x in**
14. **951 cm = x m**
15. **3520 yd = x km**
16. **7.917 ft = x in**
17. **2.917 ft = x cm**
18. **2069 g = x kg**
19. **2.125 mi = x m**
20. **25 ft = x m**

Area and Volume conversions

Area			**Volume**		
	Question	**Answer**		**Question**	**Answer**
1.	**25 cm^2**	________**in^2**	**11.**	**25 cm^3**	________**in^3**
2.	**32 in^2**	________**cm^2**	**12.**	**32 in^3**	________**cm^3**
3.	**1.25 ft^2**	________**cm^2**	**13.**	**1.25 ft^3**	________**cm^3**
4.	**4608 in^2**	________**cm^2**	**14.**	**4608 in^3**	________**cm^3**
5.	**4608 in^2**	________**ft^2**	**15.**	**4608 in^3**	________**ft^3**
6.	**8.6 ft^2**	________**cm^2**	**16.**	**8.6 ft^3**	________**cm^3**
7.	**178 cm^2**	________**in^2**	**17.**	**178 cm^3**	________**in^3**
8.	**1935.48 cm^2**	________**in^2**	**18.**	**1935.48 cm^3**	________**in^3**
9.	**1935.48 cm^2**	________**ft^2**	**19.**	**1935.48 cm^3**	________**ft^3**
10.	**1 m^2**	________**in^2**	**20.**	**1 m^3**	________**in^3**

Geometry Rules Summary for Trades

1. Straight Line – shortest line through 2 points and is equal to 180°.
2. Angle – 2 straight lines from a common point. The common point is called the vertex and the lines are called the sides of the angle.
3. Labelling Angles

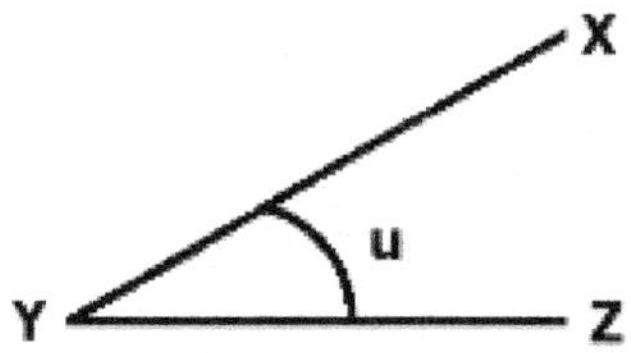

$$\measuredangle \boldsymbol{XYZ} = \measuredangle \boldsymbol{ZYX} = \measuredangle \boldsymbol{Y} = \measuredangle \boldsymbol{u}$$

If the three letter form is used the vertex letter is ALWAYS in the middle.

4. Degree – 1/360 of a circle, 1°≈1 hour (old sailing convention)
5. Minute – 1/60 of a degree
6. Second – 1/60 of a minute
7. Definitions of Angles
   i. Acute – angle is less than 90°
   ii. Obtuse – angle is greater than 90°
   iii. Right – angle is 90°
   iv. Perpendicular – lines meet at 90°
   v. Straight line - 180°
   vi. Complementary angles – add to 90°
   vii. Supplementary angles – add to 180°
8. Vertical Angles are equal

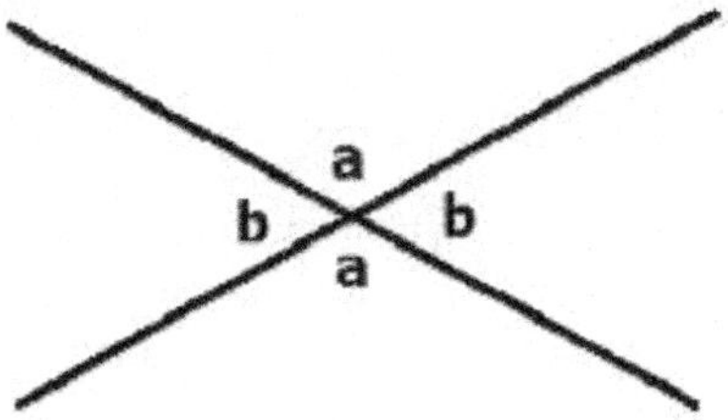

9. Angles in a triangle will add to 180°

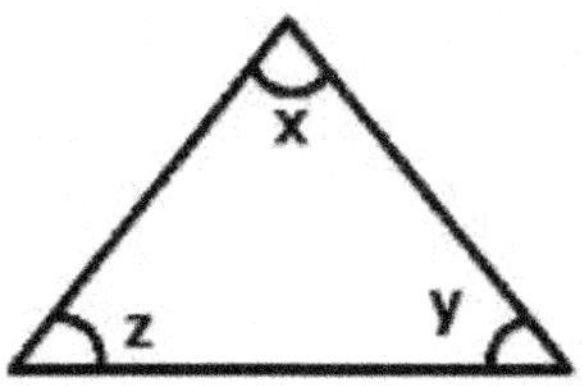

$$\measuredangle \boldsymbol{x} + \measuredangle \boldsymbol{y} + \measuredangle \boldsymbol{z} = \mathbf{180°}$$

10. Transverse Parallel Line Theorem

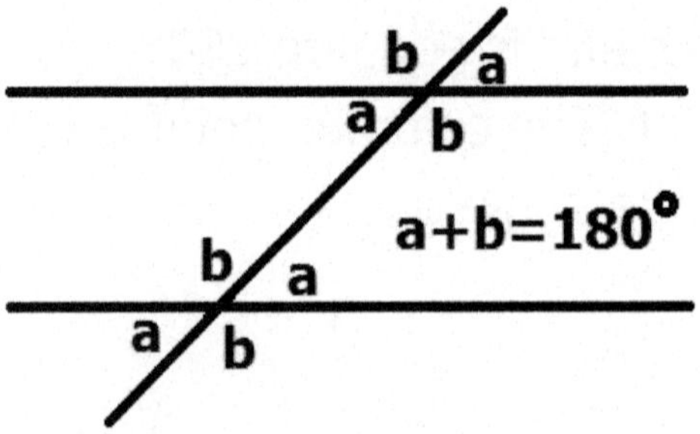

11. Congruent figures – means the figures are exactly the same
12. Similarity- the ratio of the sides are equal

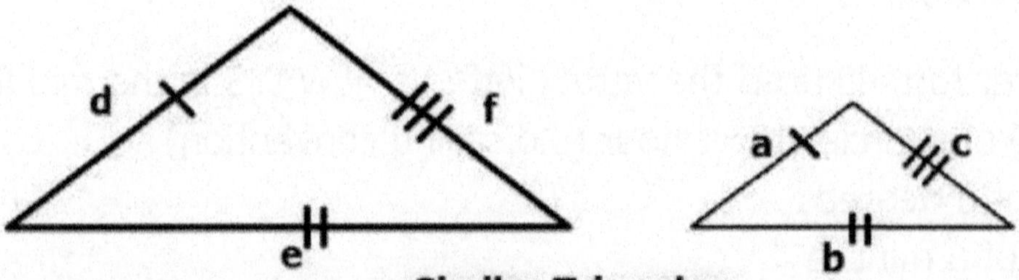

Similar Triangles

$$\textbf{Ratio of Sides}\ \frac{a}{d} = \frac{b}{e} = \frac{c}{f}$$

13. Polygon – many sided figure, all straight lines.
    Interior angles add up to (n-2)180 where n is the number of sides
    i. Vertex – where 2 lines meet
    ii. Diagonal – drawn from 1 vertex to 1 opposite
    iii. Perimeter – sum of the lengths of each side
14. Quadrilaterals – 4 straight lines, interior angles always add to 360°
    i. Square – all 4 sides are of equal length and all 4 angles are 90°
    ii. Rectangle – pairs of sides are equal in length (see chart)
    iii. Trapezoid – only 1 pair of sides are parallel lines
    iv. Parallelogram- pairs of sides are equal and parallel. A rectangle also can be considered a parallelogram.
15. Pentagon – 5 sided figure
16. Hexagon – 6 sided figure
17. Octagon – 8 sided figure

18. Areas, Perimeters and Volumes of common shapes

Figure	Perimeter	Area
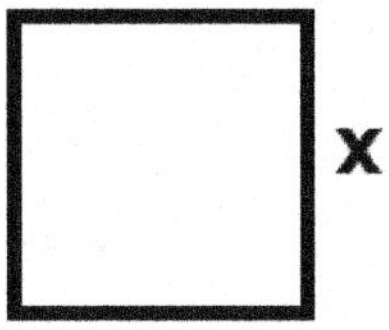 SQUARE	$P = 4x$	$A = x^2$
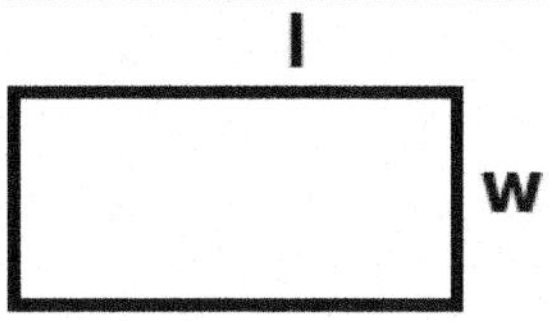 RECTANGLE	$P = 2l + 2w$	$A = lw$
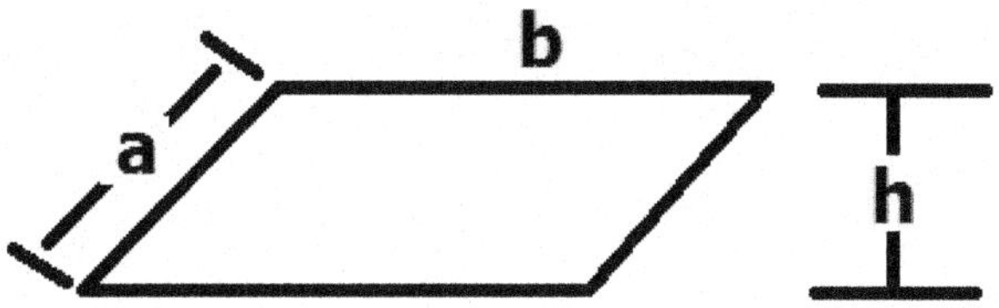 PARALLELOGRAM	$P = 2a + 2b$	$A = bh$
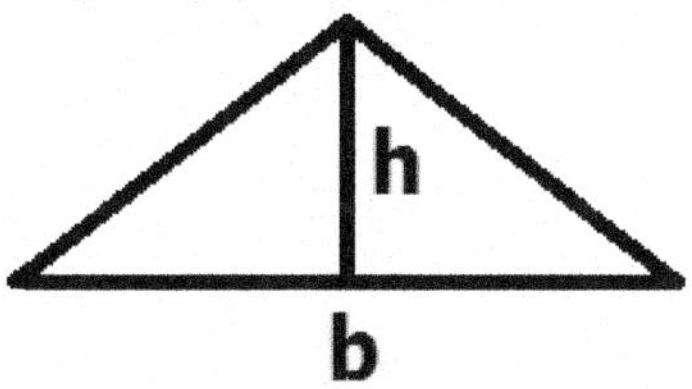 TRIANGLE	Sum of sides	$A = \frac{1}{2}bh$
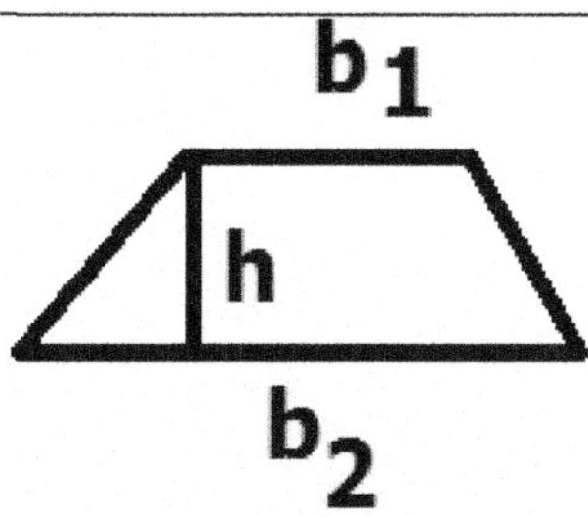 TRAPEZOID	Sum of sides	$A = \frac{h}{2}(b_1 + b_2)$
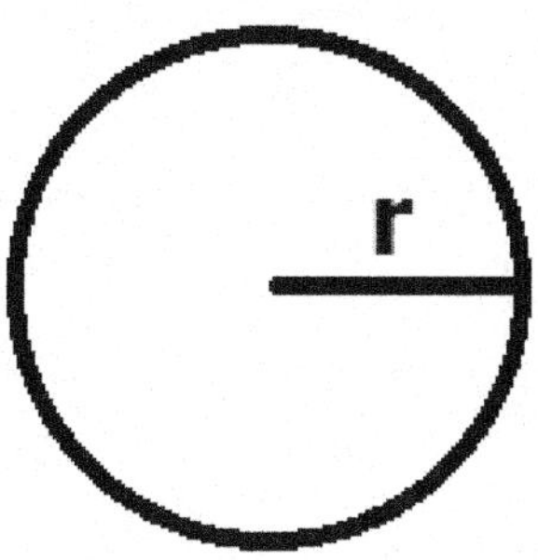 $d = 2r$ CIRCLE	$C = 2\pi r = \pi d$	$A = \pi r^2 = \frac{\pi d^2}{4}$

Advanced Geometry Figures

<table>
<tr>
<td>
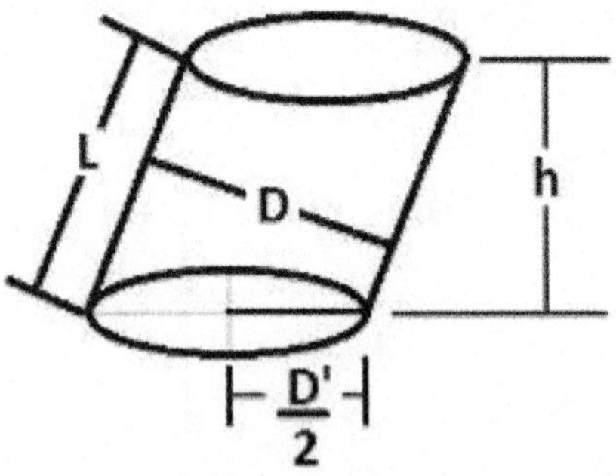

</td>
<td>

Oblique Circular Cylinder

$V = Base\ x\ Altitude$

$V = \pi r^2 h$

$TSA = 2\pi rL + 2\pi \frac{D'}{2} r$

</td>
</tr>
<tr>
<td>
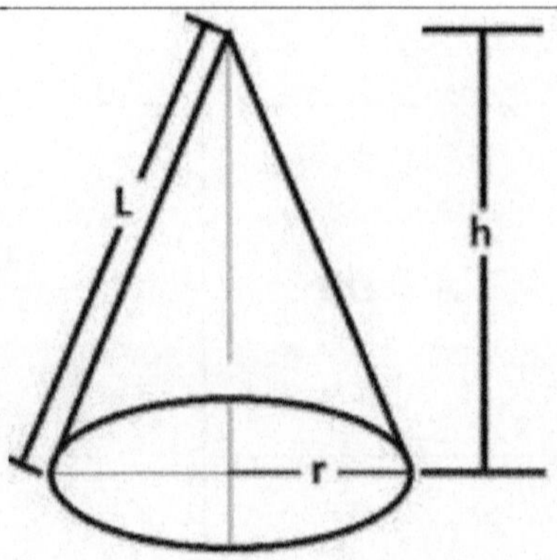

</td>
<td>

Right Circular Cone

$V = \frac{1}{3} x\ Base\ x\ Altitude$

$V = \frac{\pi r^2}{3} h$

$TSA = \pi r (r + L)$

</td>
</tr>
<tr>
<td>
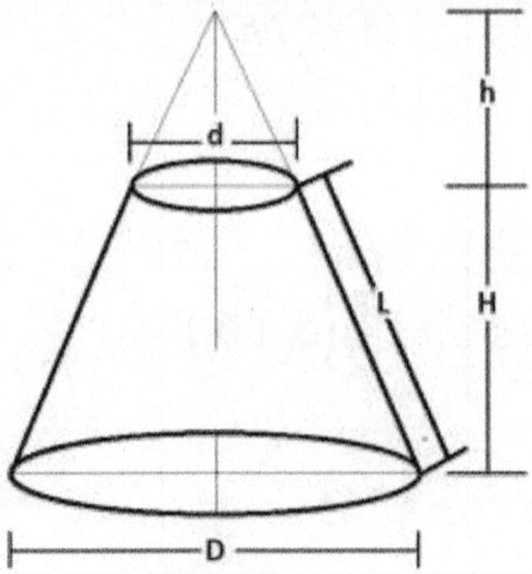

</td>
<td>

Frustum of a Right Circular Cone

$V = \frac{\pi H}{12} \left[D^2 + dD + d^2 \right]$

$TSA = \pi L (R + r)$

</td>
</tr>
<tr>
<td>
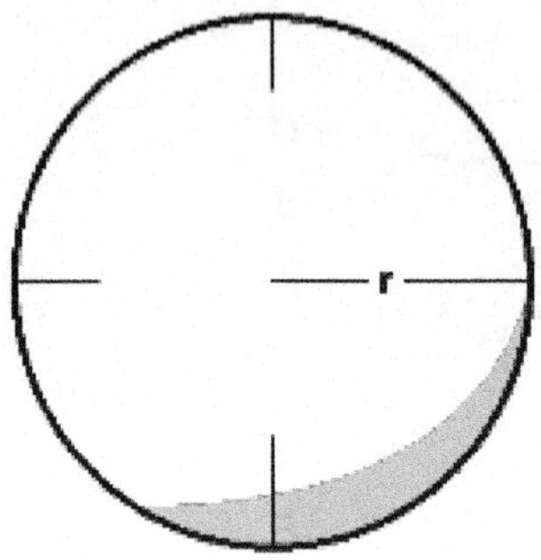

</td>
<td>

Sphere

$V = \frac{4}{3} \pi r^3 = \frac{\pi}{6} d^3$

$S.A. = 4\pi r^2$

</td>
</tr>
</table>

Surface Areas and Volumes Cont'd

Figure	S.A. and Vol.
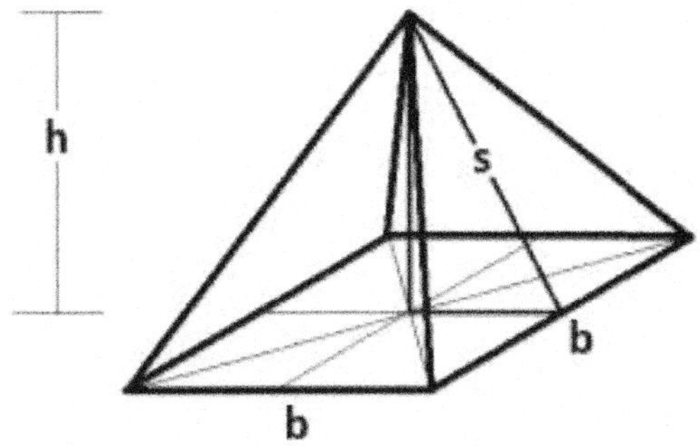	**Square Based Pyramid** **S.A.** $= 2bs + b^2$ **s = slant height** $V = \frac{1}{3}b^2h$
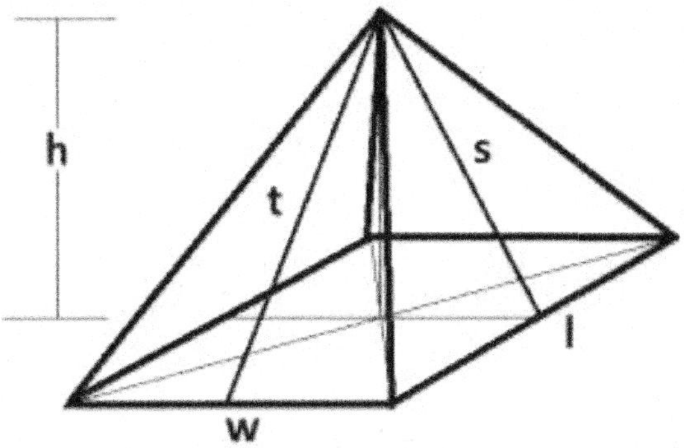	**Rectangular Based Pyramid** **S.A.** $= wt + ls + wl$ **s,t = slant heights** $V = \frac{1}{3}lwh$
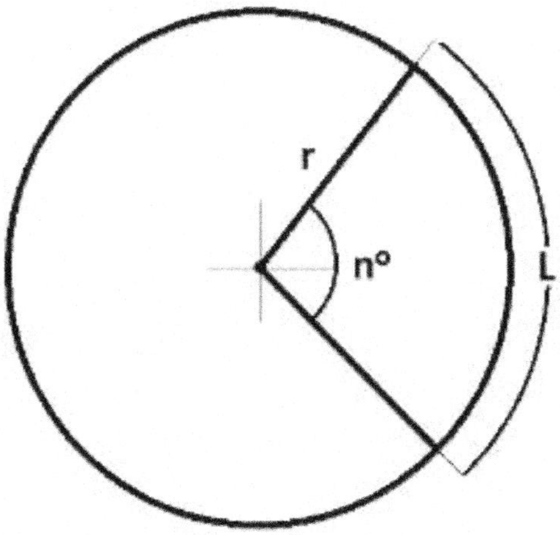	**Length of an Arc** $L = \frac{n^\circ}{360^\circ} x 2\pi r$

Volumes of some common shapes

Figure Name	Volume	Surface Area
Cube 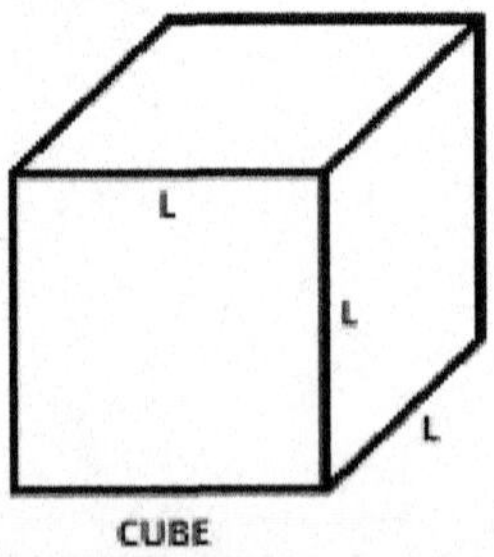	$V = L^3$	$S.A. = 6L^2$
Cylinder 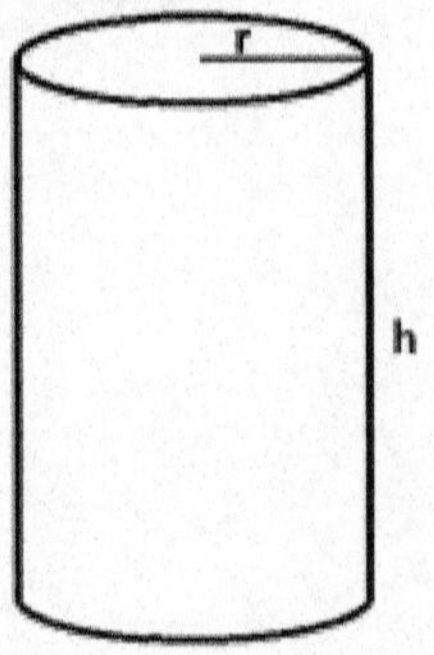	$V = \pi r^2 h$	$S.A. = 2\pi r^2 + Ch$ where $C = 2\pi r$ OR $S.A. = 2\pi r(r+h)$
Rectangular Tank 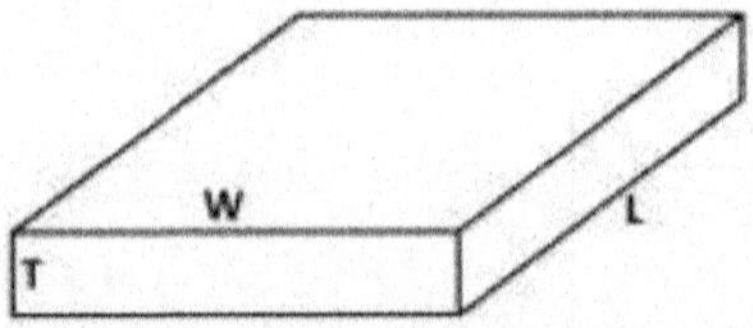	$V = T \cdot W \cdot L$	$S.A. = 2(W \cdot L + W \cdot T + L \cdot T)$
Solid Parallelogram 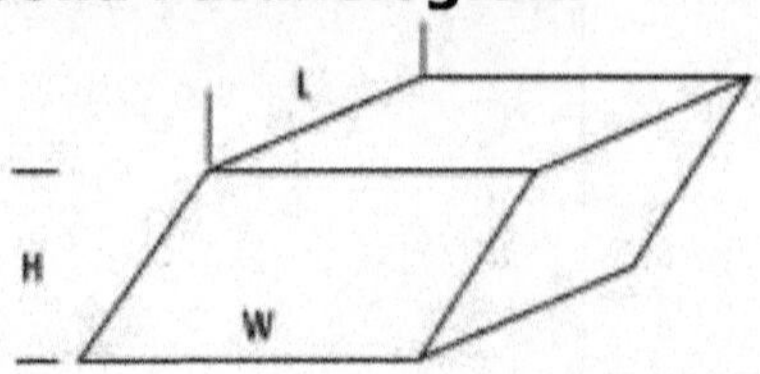	$V = H \cdot W \cdot L$	**More information needed**
Semicircular Tank 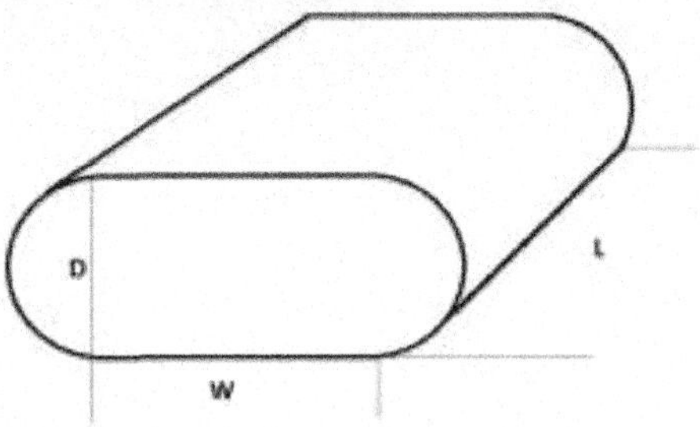	$V = \pi \frac{D^2}{4} L + D \cdot W \cdot L$	$S.A. = L(\pi D + 2W) + 2\left(\pi \frac{D^2}{4} + DW\right)$

19. Special triangles

i. Equilateral – all sides and angles are equal (see fig. 1)

ii. Isosceles – two sides are equal, and the angles opposite these sides are equal (see fig. 2)

iii. Acute – all angles are less than 90°

iv. Scalene – no sides are equal and all angles are less than 90°

v. Obtuse – one angle is greater than 90°

vi. Right – one angle is 90°

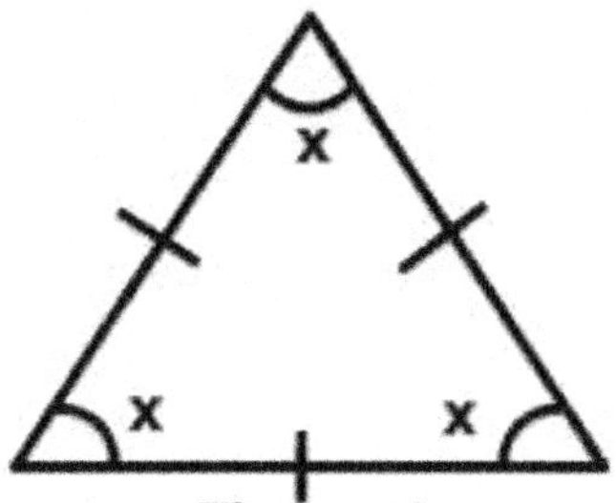

Figure 1

Figure 2

20. Right (angle) Triangle – one angle is always 90°

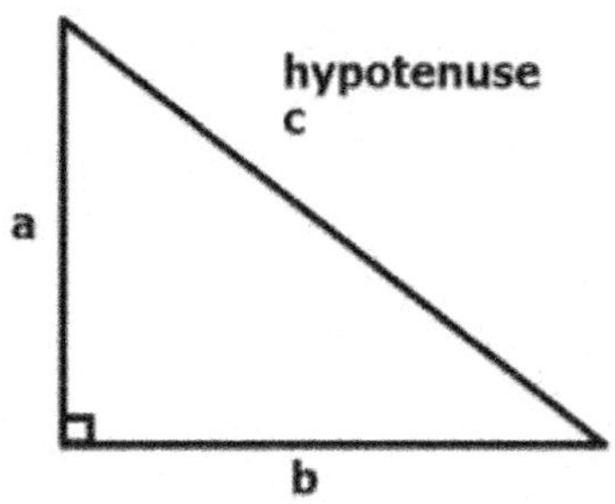

$$\boldsymbol{c} = \sqrt{\boldsymbol{a}^2 + \boldsymbol{b}^2}$$

$$\boldsymbol{a} = \sqrt{\boldsymbol{c}^2 - \boldsymbol{b}^2}$$

$$\boldsymbol{b} = \sqrt{\boldsymbol{c}^2 - \boldsymbol{a}^2}$$

21. Area of any triangle

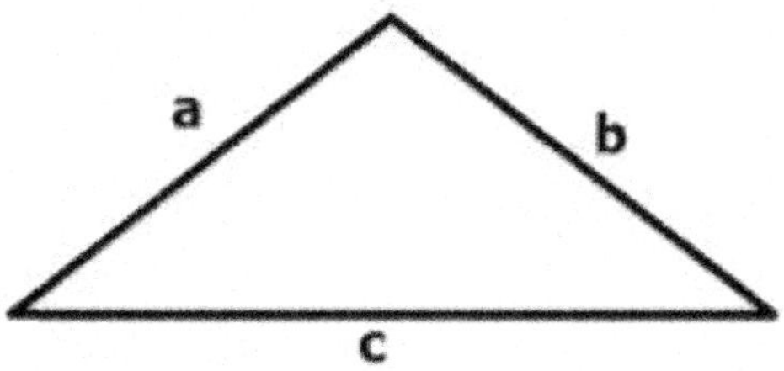

$$\boldsymbol{s} = \frac{\boldsymbol{a}+\boldsymbol{b}+\boldsymbol{c}}{\mathbf{2}}$$

$$\boldsymbol{A} = \sqrt{\boldsymbol{s}(\boldsymbol{s}-\boldsymbol{a})(\boldsymbol{s}-\boldsymbol{b})(\boldsymbol{s}-\boldsymbol{c})}$$

22. Hexagon

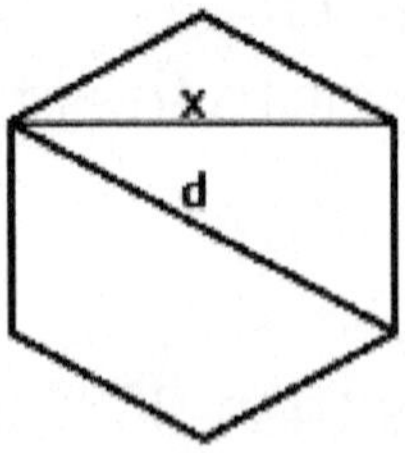

$$Area = \frac{3a^2\sqrt{3}}{2} \approx 2.598a^2$$
$$d = 1.1547x$$
$$x = 0.86603d$$

23. Exterior Angles

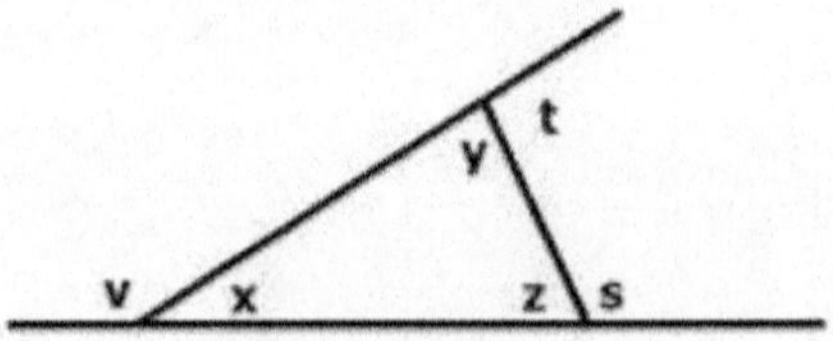

$$\measuredangle s = \measuredangle x + \measuredangle y$$
$$\measuredangle t = \measuredangle x + \measuredangle z$$
$$\measuredangle v = \measuredangle y + \measuredangle z$$

24. Interior angles of a triangle = 180°.

25. Central and Vertex Angles

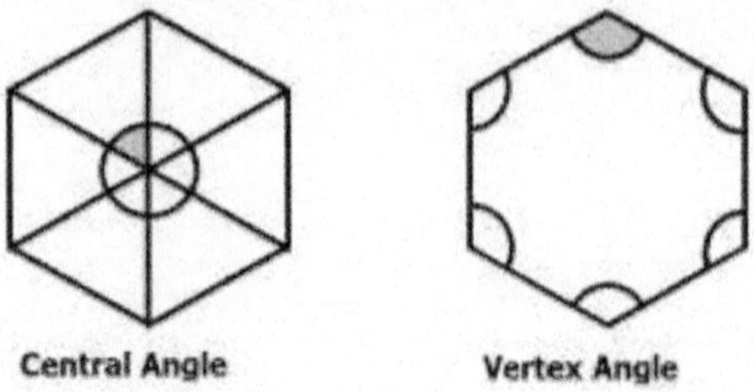

n = number of sides

central angle = $\frac{360^\circ}{n}$

vertex angle = interior angle = $(n-2)\cdot 180^\circ$

26. Projections in Triangles

i. Interior

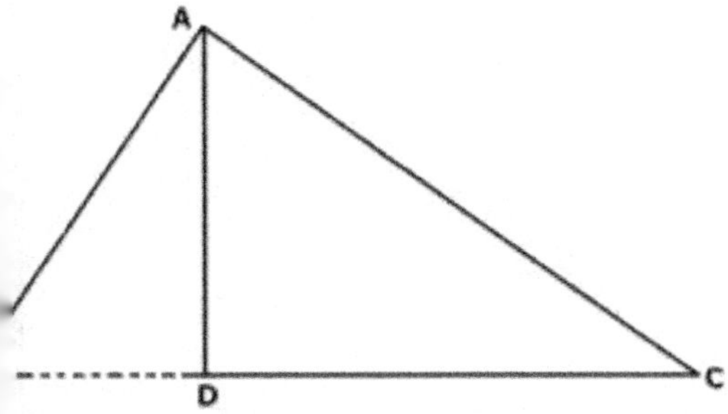

Projection of AB onto base (BD)

$$BD = \frac{AB^2 + BC^2 - AC^2}{2xBC}$$

ii. Exterior

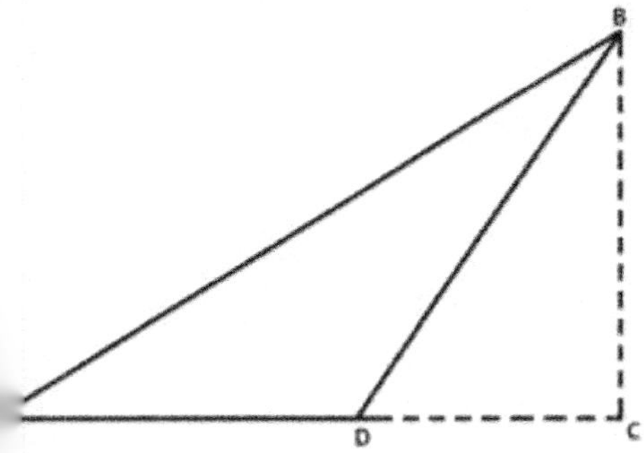

$$CD = \frac{AB^2 - AD^2 - BD^2}{2xAD}$$

27. Definitions and Rules for Circles

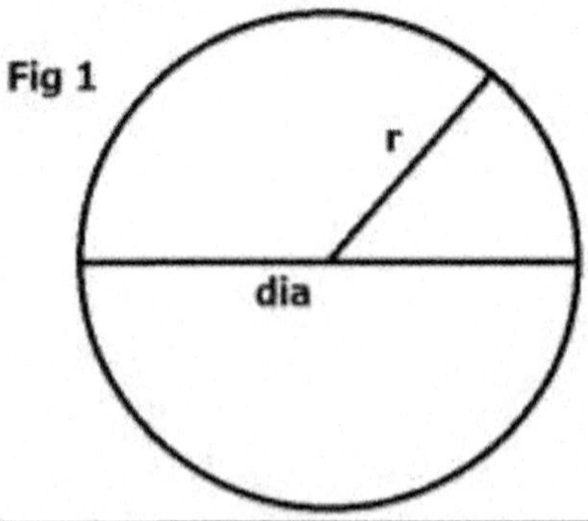	**The *radius* (r or R) is ½ the *diameter* of the circle. The diameter is always drawn through the center.**
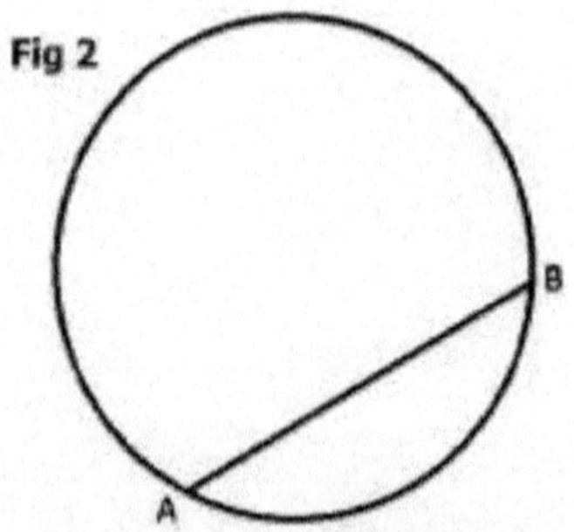	**The line shown here is a *chord*.** **It is labelled the same as a line segment.** $\overline{AB}$ **is the chord shown here.**
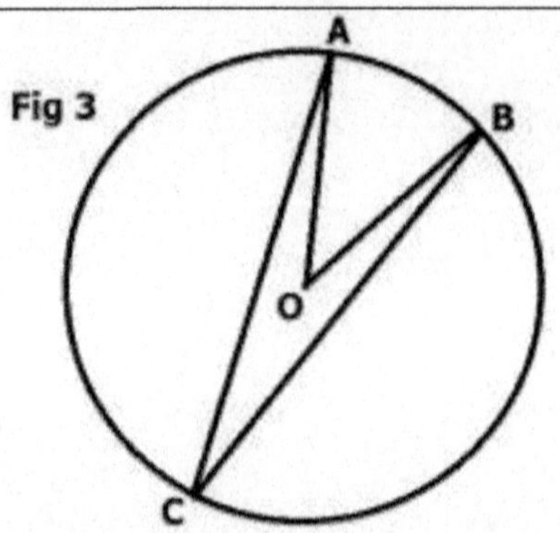	**Central angle is always double the inscribed angle on the same minor arc.** $\angle AOB = 2x\angle ACB$ AB is the minor arc that both angles touch.
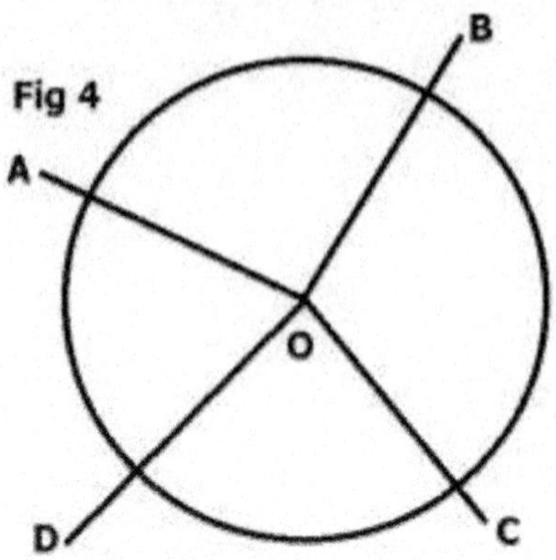	**The ratio of central angles is equal to the ratio of their minor arcs.** $\frac{\angle AOB}{\angle BOC} = \frac{AD}{BC}$
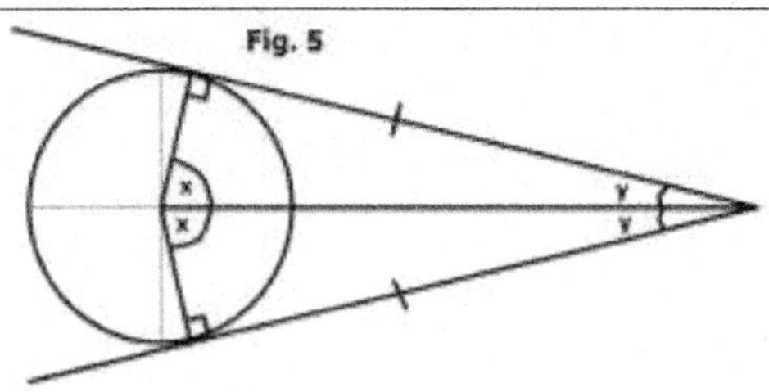	**When two tangents from a circle are drawn to a common exterior point the two triangles are identical (congruent).**

Table Continued

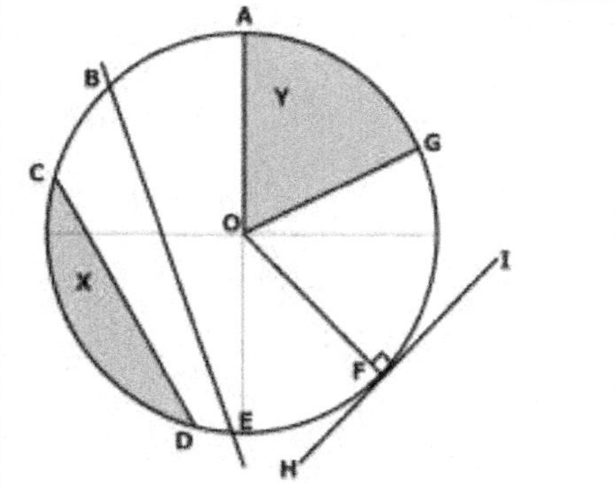	1. *AG* and $\angle AOG$ are the boundaries of a <u>SECTOR</u>. 2. Area X is called a <u>SEGMENT</u> bounded by the <u>CHORD</u> $\overline{CD}$ and *DC*. 3. $\overline{BE}$ is called a <u>*SECANT*</u>, and $\overline{HI}$ is called a <u>*TANGENT*</u>. 4. Radius always meets a tangent at 90° 5. Tangents only touch at one point.
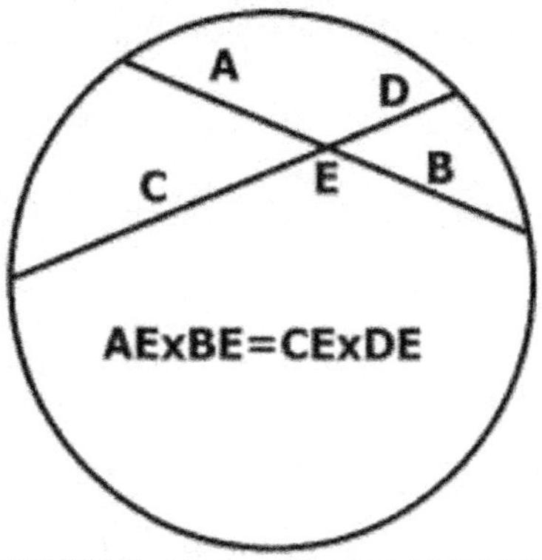	**Intersecting Chords** If two chords meet at a common point inside the circle, then the products of their parts are equal.
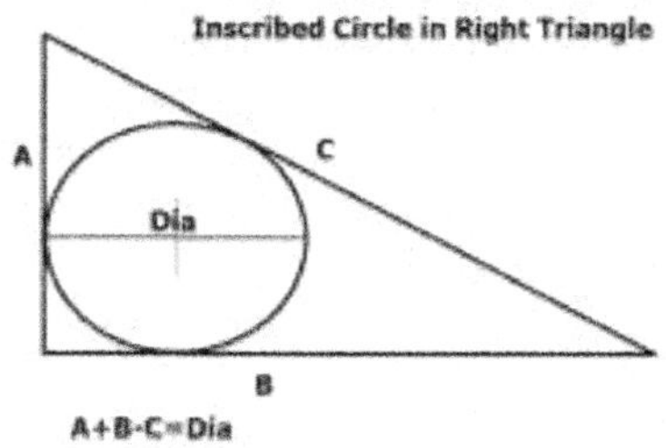	The diameter of a circle inscribed inside a right angle triangle is equal to the sum of the legs minus the hypotenuse. $A + B - C =$ Dia
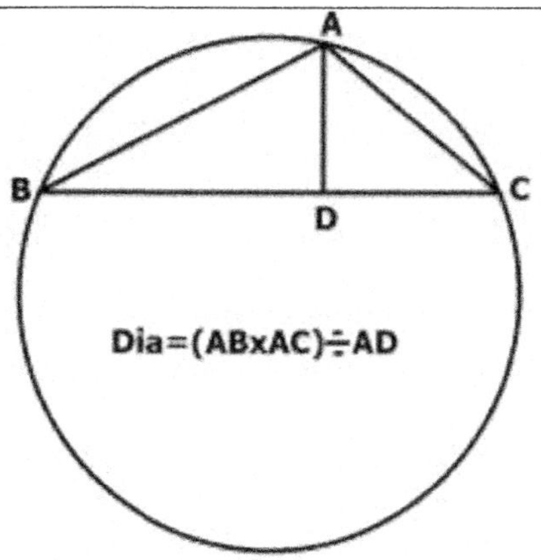	If a triangle is inscribed inside a circle and the altitude is given, then the diameter of the circle can be calculated.
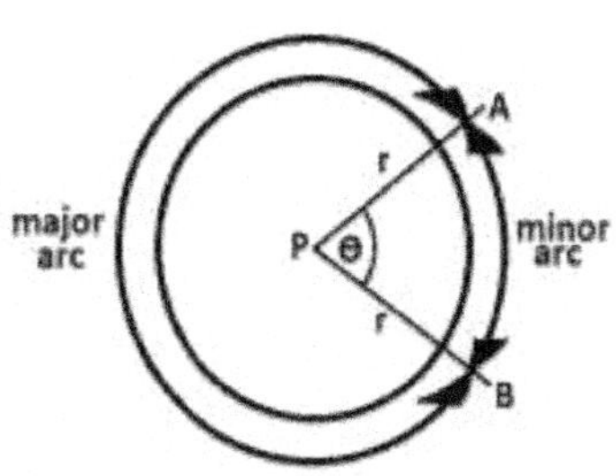	Shows the relationship between minor and major arcs.

Table continued

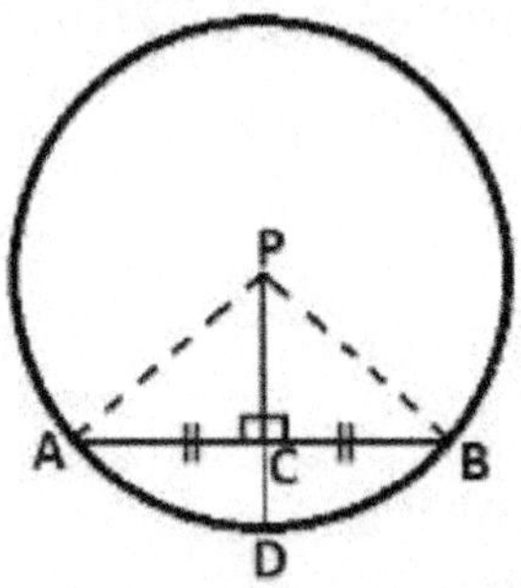	**A radius that is drawn perpendicular to a chord will always bisect (split in half) the chord.** $\overline{AC} = \overline{CB}$
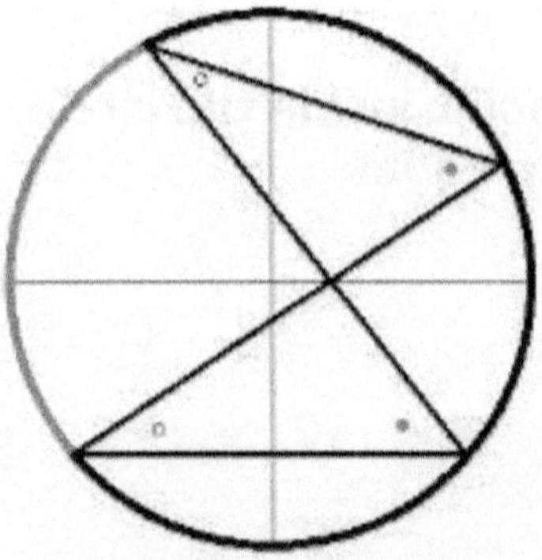	**If two (or more) inscribed angles touch the same arc, then these angles are congruent (equal).**
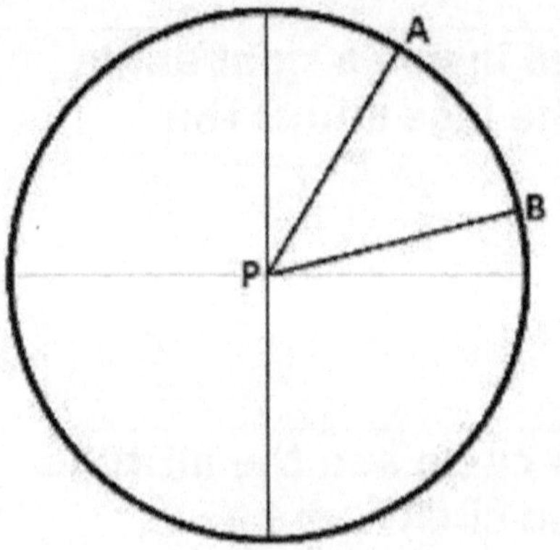	**The ratio of a central angle to the full circle is the same as the ratio between the minor arc and the circumference.** **i.e.** **Given:** $r = 2, \quad C = 12.5664, \quad \angle APB = 40^\circ, \quad AB = 1.3963$ $\frac{40^\circ}{360^\circ} = \frac{1.3963}{12.5664} = 0.1111$ **This can be used then to find a missing angle or arc length.**
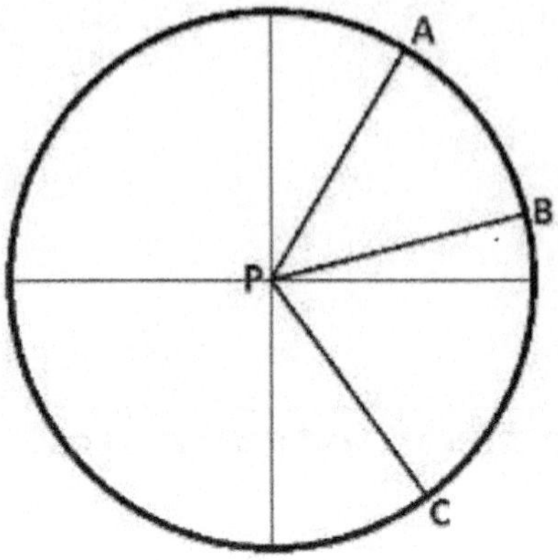	**Arc Addition** $\angle APB + \angle BPC = \angle APC$ $AB + BC = AC$

Volume to Mass Conversions

Volume of material to weight conversion

Example:

Determine the weight of a steel bar that measures 2"x2"x16".

Answer: V=LxWxD=64in^3

Weight =Volume x Weight Density=64 in^{3}x0.2836lbs/ in^3=18.1504 lb

Example 2

Determine the weight of a copper tank made from ¼" plate given the drawing and dimensions below. Note ¼"=0.653cm

The top plate has a 8 cm radius fill hole cut out.

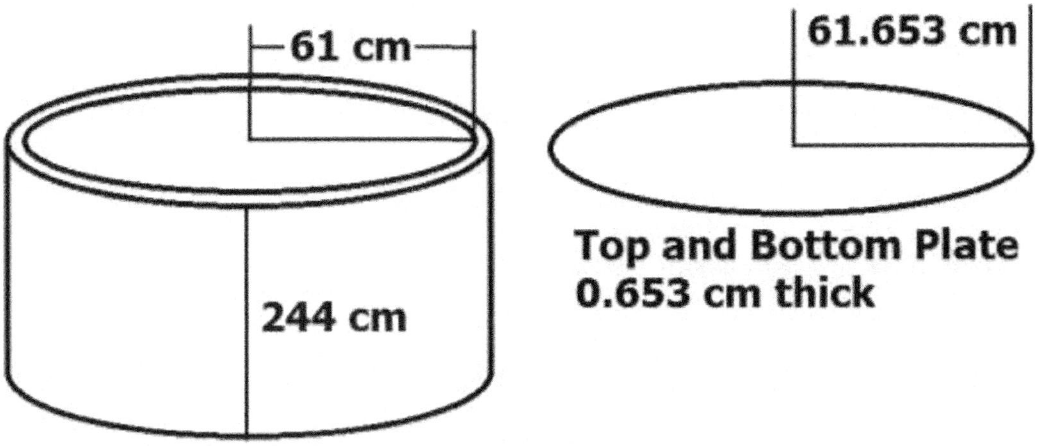

Answer:

Main Body (Side)=$Vol_{O.D.} - Vol_{I.D.}$

$= \pi R^2 h - \pi r^2 h$

$= \pi (61.653)^2 x244 - \pi (61)^2 x244$

$= 2913722.093 - 2852327.368$

$= \underline{\underline{61394.72459 cm^3}}$

Vol bottom plate

$= \pi r^2 h \qquad h = 0.653cm$ **thick**

$= \pi (61.653)^2 x0.653$

$= \underline{\underline{7797.789044 cm^3}}$

Vol top plate=Vol bottom plate - fill hole

Fill hole=$\pi r^2 h = \pi (8)^2 x0.653$

$= 131.2934402 cm^3$

Top Plate=$7797.789044 - 131.2934402 cm^3$

$= \underline{\underline{7666.495604 cm^3}}$

Total volume

$V_T = 61394.72459 + 7797.789044 + 7666.495604$

$= \underline{\underline{76859 cm^3}}$

Weight=V_T **x Weight Density (copper)**

$= 76859\ cm^3 \times 8.93 \, g/cm^3 = 686350.87g = \underline{\underline{686.4kg}}$

The tank will weigh 686.4 kg (which approximately =1538 lb).

Convert each of the following, 2 decimal places for accuracy.

For metals with a range of values choose the lowest number.

1. **1437 cm^3 of aluminum (Al)** ____________________
2. **3.125 ft^3 of brass 60/40** ____________________
3. **4168 in^3 of tungsten** ____________________
4. **1.89 m^3 of cast iron** ____________________
5. **27.75 m^3 of stainless steel** ____________________

Calculate the volume for each drawing and convert to the appropriate weight.

6. **What is the weight (in kg) of the steel box?**

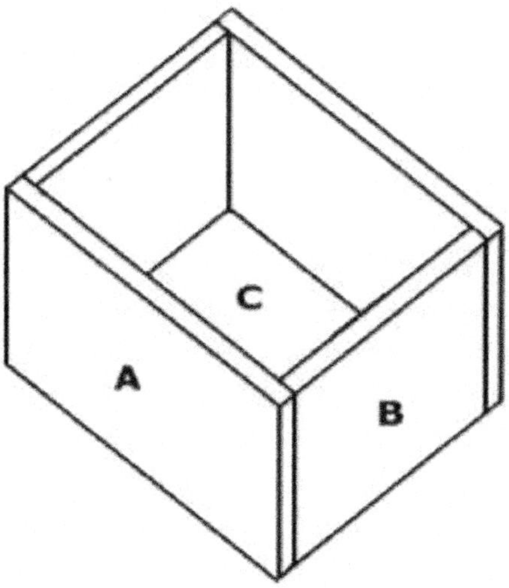

Dimensions

Plate A 70cmx40cmx1.27cm

Plate B 40cmx40cmx1.27cm

Plate C 70cmx40cmx1.27cm

Volume to Weight Conversion SHEET 2

Convert each of the following, 2 decimal places for accuracy.

For metals with a range of values choose the lowest number.

1. 2.875 m^3 of aluminum (Al) ____________________
2. 3.125 ft^3 of iron ____________________
3. 4168 in^3 of wrought iron ____________________
4. 1.89 m^3 of yellow brass ____________________
5. 27.75 m^3 of titanium ____________________
6. Calculate the volume of steel plate needed for the bin below if ¼" stainless steel is used. Assume there is a bottom plate.
7. What is the weight (in lbs) of the stainless steel box?

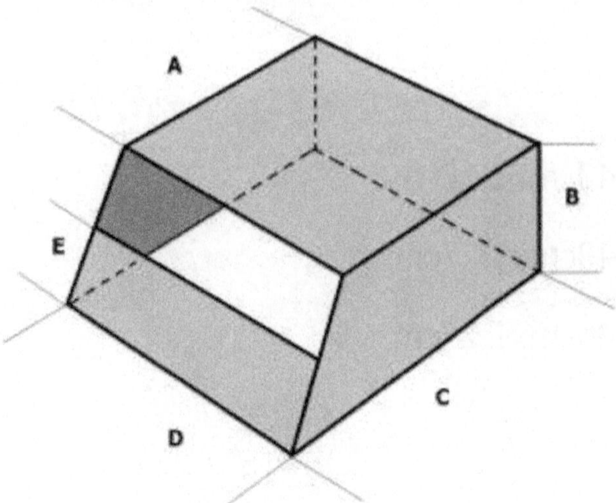

A	22 in
B	19 in
C	36 in
D	22 in
E	10 in

Mass Densities of some metals

Metal or Alloy	Density g/cm^3	Density kg/m^3	Density lbs/in^3	Density lbs/ft^3
Aluminum	2.712	2712	0.09798	169.23
Aluminum bronze (3-10% Al)	7.7-8.7	7700-8700	0.27818-0.3143	480.48-542.88
Beryllium Copper	8.1-8.25	8100-8250	0.29263-0.29805	505.44-514.8
Brass-rolled and Drawn	8.43-8.73	8430-8730	0.30455-0.31539	526.03-544.75
Brass 60/40	8.52	8520	0.3078	531.65
Bronze-lead	7.7-8.7	7700-8700	0.27818-0.3143	480.48-542.88
Cast Iron	6.8-7.8	6800-7800	0.24566-0.28179	424.32-486.72
Copper	8.93	8930	0.32261	557.23
Iron	7.85	7850	0.28359	489.84
Lead	11.34	11340	0.40968	707.62
Light Al alloy	2.56-2.8	2560-2800	0.09249-0.10116	159.74-174.72
Light Mg alloy	1.76-1.87	1760-1870	0.06358-0.06756	109.82-116.69
Phosphor Bronze	8.9	8900	0.32153	555.36
Red Brass	8.746	8746	0.31597	545.75
Stainless Steel	7.48-8	7480-8000	0.27023-0.28902	466.75-499.2
Steel	7.85	7850	0.2836	489.84
Titanium	4.5	4500	0.16257	280.8
Tungsten	19.6	19600	0.70809	1223.04
White metal	7.1	7100	0.2565	443.04
Wrought iron	7.75	7750	0.27998	483.6
Yellow Brass	8.47	8470	0.30599	528.53

$$1\,{}^{kg}\!/_{m^3} = 0.0624\,{}^{lbs}\!/_{ft^2} = 0.000036127\,{}^{lbs}\!/_{in^2} = 0.001\,{}^{g}\!/_{cm^3}$$

Block 2

1. **Triangles – see Geometry Rules Summary**
2. **Quadrilaterals and Polygons**

Types of Quadrilaterals

Type	**Properties**
Square 	- **All sides are equal** - **All angles are equal** - **Diagonals are equal in length**
Rectangle 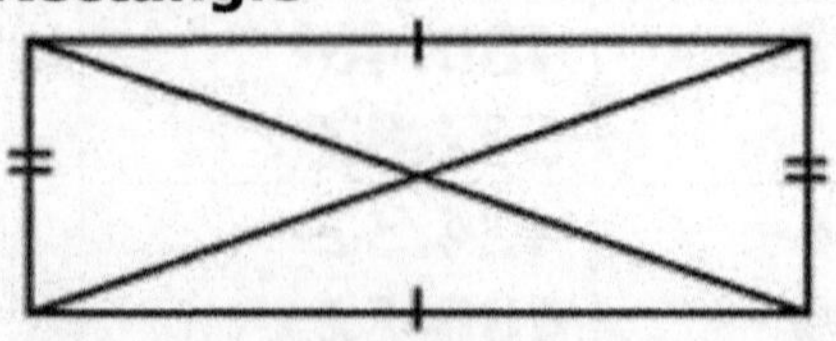	- **Opposite sides are equal in length** - **All angles are equal** - **Diagonals are equal in length**
Parallelogram 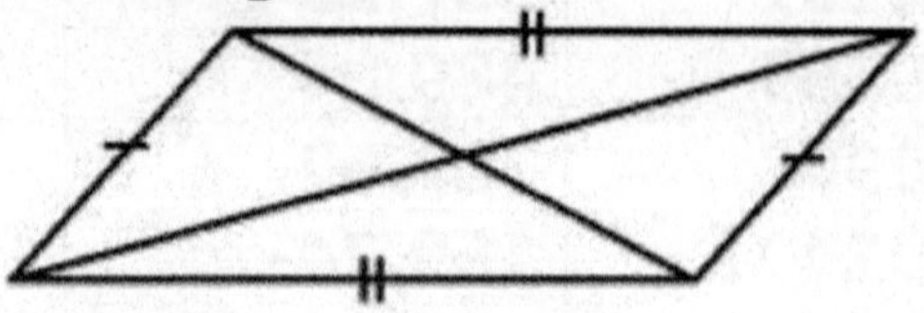	- **Opposite sides are parallel** - **The side pairs are equal in length** - **The diagonals are NOT equal in length** - **The diagonals bisect each other**
Rhombus 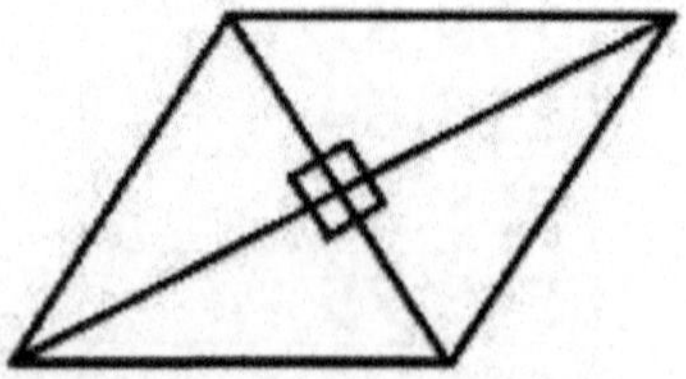	- **All sides are equal** - **All angles are equal** - **Diagonals are equal** - **Diagonals meet at 90°**
Trapezoid 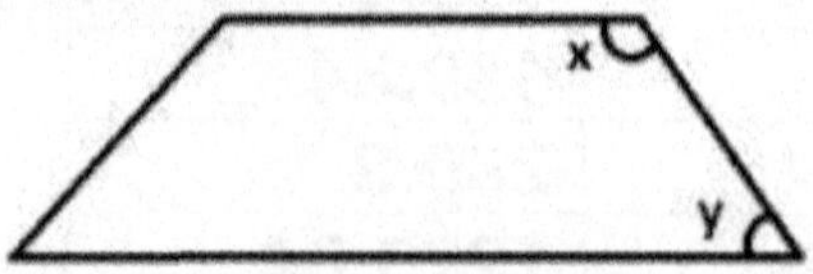	- **One pair of sides are parallel**
Isosceles Trapezoid 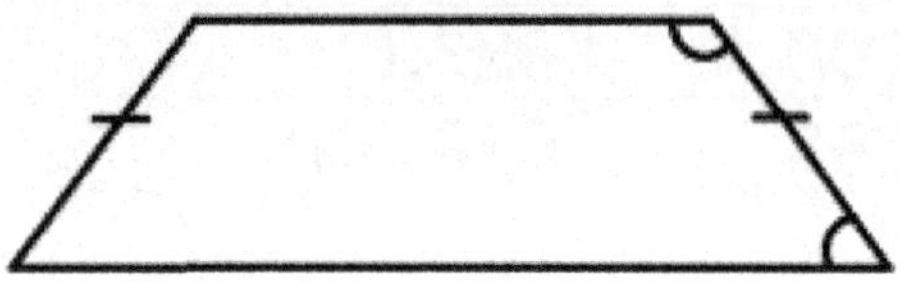	- **One pair are equal in length** - **Angles along side are supplemental** $\angle x + \angle y = 180°$ - **Diagonals are equal in length**

Polygons

A polygon is literally a multisided figure.

Central angle - $\frac{360°}{n}$ n = number of sides

Vertex Angle (interior) - $\frac{(n-2)x180°}{n}$ = single vertex angle

$(n-2)x180°$ = sum of all vertex angles

Vertex angle (exterior) - 360° – interior vertex angle

Here are a few common polygons to demonstrate the math.

Type	Central Angle	Vertex Angle
Pentagon **n=5** 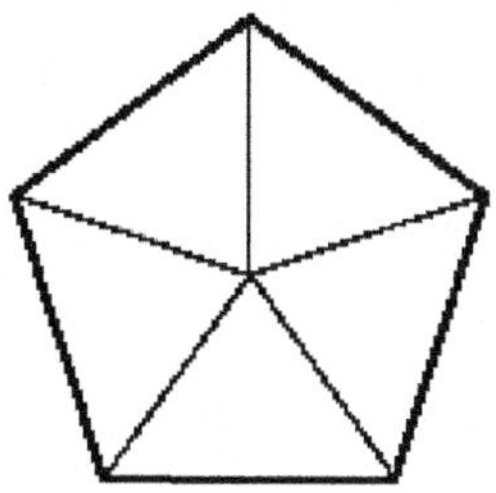	$\frac{360}{5} = 72°$	$(5-2)180° = 540°$ total sum $\frac{540°}{5} = 108°$ vertex angle $360° - 108° = 252°$ exterior vertex angle
Hexagon **n=6** 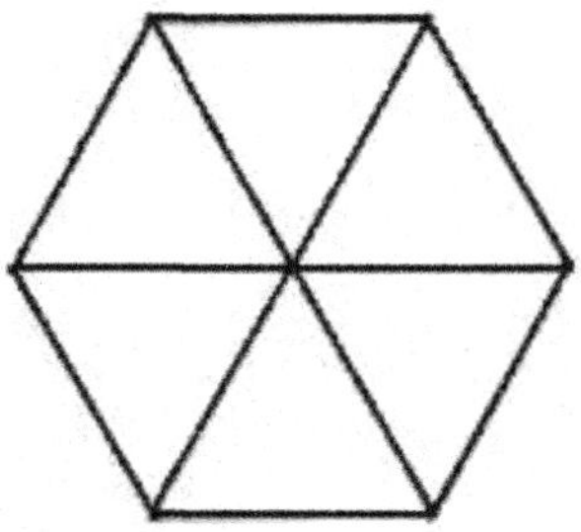	$\frac{360°}{6} = 60°$	$(6-2)180 = 720°$ $\frac{720°}{6} = 120°$ $360° - 120° = 240°$
Octagon **n=8** 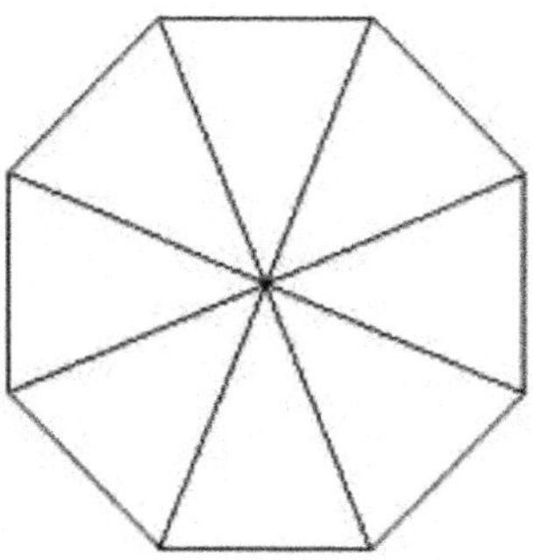	$\frac{360°}{8} = 45°$	$(8-2)180 = 1080°$ $\frac{1080°}{8} = 135°$ $360° - 135° = 225°$

3. Simple Algebra

i. Using Equations

Note: Multiplication signs (x) are rarely or never used in algebra to avoid confusion with the letter 'x'. Here are the ways to indicate a multiplication in algebra.

$$\left.\begin{array}{ll}\text{no sign} & 2y \\ \text{dot} & 2\cdot y \\ \text{bracket} & 2(y)\end{array}\right\}$$

Every case means the same thing "2 times y".

Sample – Find the perimeter (P) if length is 14" and the width is 10".

$$P = 2\ell + 2w$$
$$P = 2(14") + 2(10")$$
$$P = 28" + 20"$$
$$P = 48"$$

ii. Rearranging Equations

This is done by doing the reverse of the order of operations and following the rules outlined below.

Rules of Equations

A. If the same number is added to equal numbers then the sums are also equal.

$3\mathbf{x} - 17 = 4$ **Because of the equal sign the 'number' on the left is identical to the 'number' on the right.**

$$3\mathbf{x} - 17 = 4$$
$$+17 \quad +17$$ **The new numbers in the therefore statement are now also equal.**
$$\therefore 3\mathbf{x} = 21$$

B. If the same number is subtracted from equal numbers the remainders remain equal.

$$\mathbf{x} + 7 = 8$$
$$-7 \quad -7$$
$$\therefore \mathbf{x} = 1$$

C. If equal numbers are multiplied by the same number the products are still equal.

$$\frac{x}{2} = 3$$

$$2 \cdot \frac{x}{2} = 3 \cdot 2$$

$$x = 6$$

D. If equal numbers are divided by the same number the quotients are still equal.

$$3x = 21$$

$$\frac{3x}{3} = \frac{21}{3}$$

$$\therefore x = 7$$

Sample – Find the length if the width is 10" and the perimeter is 48".

$P = 2\ell + 2w$

$48 = 2\ell + 2(10)$

$48 = 2\ell + 20$ subtract 20 from BOTH sides

$28 = 2\ell$ divide BOTH sides by '2'

$14 = \ell$

$\therefore \ell = 14"$

Because of the rules above, the equal sign must be treated as carved in stone. Whatever is done to one side MUST BE DONE to the other side.

Here are some more samples.

Sample 2 - If the sum of vertex angles is 1440°, how many sides does the polygon have?

$(n-2)180 = 1440$ first divide both sides by 180

$$\frac{(n-2)\cancel{180}}{\cancel{180}} = \frac{1440}{180} = \frac{\cancel{180} \cdot 8}{\cancel{180}}$$

$n - 2 = 8$ add '2' to both sides

n=10

Therefore, the polygon has 10 sides (decagon).

Sample 3 – If the area of a trapezoid is 160 square cm, has a height of 10 cm and one side is 14 cm long, how long is the other side?

Area of Trapezoid

$A = \frac{h}{2}(b_1 + b_2)$ Fill in the values that you know

$160cm^2 = \frac{10}{2}(14 + b_2)$

$160cm^2 = 5(14 + b_2)$ divide both sides by '5'

$\frac{160}{5} = \frac{5(14 + b_2)}{5}$

$32 = 14 + b_2$ subtract 14 from both sides

$b_2 = 18cm$

Rearranging Formulas Practice

1. $P = 2L + 2W$ **P=24cm, L=8cm find W**

2. $A = \frac{bh}{2}$ **A = 21 in^2, b = 6in find h**

3. $C = 2\pi r$ **C=31.416cm, find r**

4. $Q = 0.7ELT$ **E = 21, L = 4.2, T = 0.125 find Q**

5. $S = \pi rs$ **find s if S = 4000 and r = 462**

6. $C = \frac{5}{9}(F - 32)$ **find F if C=27**

7. $A = \frac{H}{2}(B + D)$ **find B if A = 675 cm^2, H = 27 cm and D = 30 cm**

8. $V = \pi r^2 L$ **find r if V = 95425.88 cm^3, L=135 cm**

Geometry Practice Questions

Each question shows the solution to a sample value followed by practice questions. The drawings are not to scale.

1. **Given the figure below, solve for the missing value(s).**

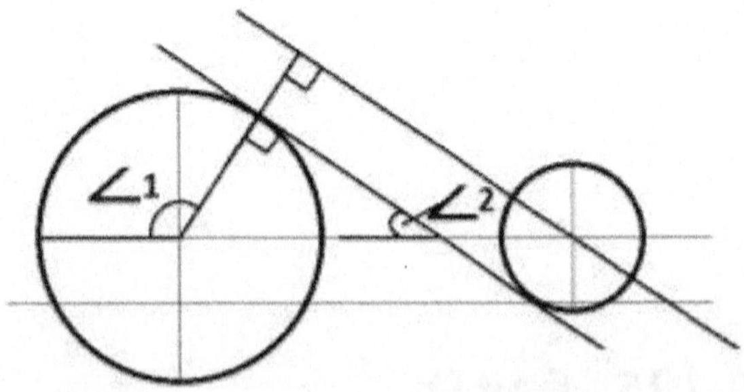

Sample

$\angle 1 = 143°$
$\angle 2 = ?$

Solution:

$180° - 143° = 37°$
$\angle 2 = 180° - (90° + 37°) = \underline{53°}$

Alternate solution:

The exterior angle to a triangle is equal to the sum of the interior opposite angles.

$143° = 90° + \angle 2$
$\angle 2 = 143° - 90° = \underline{53°}$

Questions:

	$\angle 1$	$\angle 2$
1.	**131°**	
2.	**133°**	
3.	**139°**	
4.	**141°**	

2. **Given the figure below, solve for the missing value(s).**

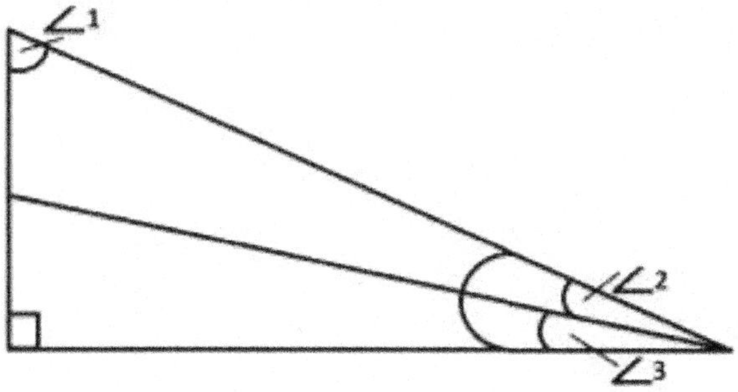

Sample

$\angle 1 = 54^\circ \quad \angle 2 = 23^\circ$

$\text{call}(\angle 2 + \angle 3) = \angle 4$

$180^\circ - (90^\circ + \angle 1) = \angle 4$

$180^\circ - (90^\circ + 54^\circ) = \angle 4 = 36^\circ$

$\angle 4 = \angle 2 + \angle 3$

$\angle 4 - \angle 2 = 36^\circ - 23^\circ = \underline{13^\circ = \angle 3}$

Questions:

$\angle 2 \equiv 23^\circ$

	$\angle 1$	$\angle 3$
1.	**58°**	
2.	**61°**	
3.	**65°**	
4.	**52°**	

3. Given the following figure, solve for the missing value(s).

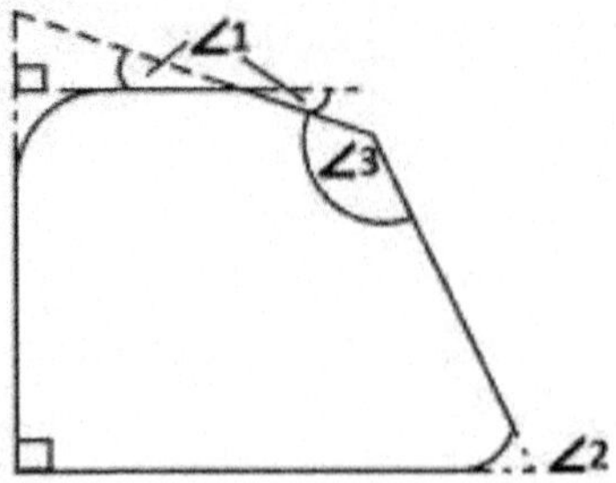

Note: the dotted lines were added for the solution.

Sample

$\angle 1 = 38°$ $\angle 2 = 58°$ $\angle 3 = ?$

Solution:

Use the polygon interior angle sum formula.

$(n-2)180°$
$= (4-2)180° = 360°$
$90° - \angle 1 = 90° - 38° = 52°$
$\angle 3 = 360° - (52° + 90° + 58°) = \underline{160°}$

Questions

$\angle 2 \equiv 58°$

	∠1	∠3
1.	**26°**	
2.	**28°**	
3.	**34°**	
4.	**36°**	

4. Given the following figure, solve for the missing value(s).

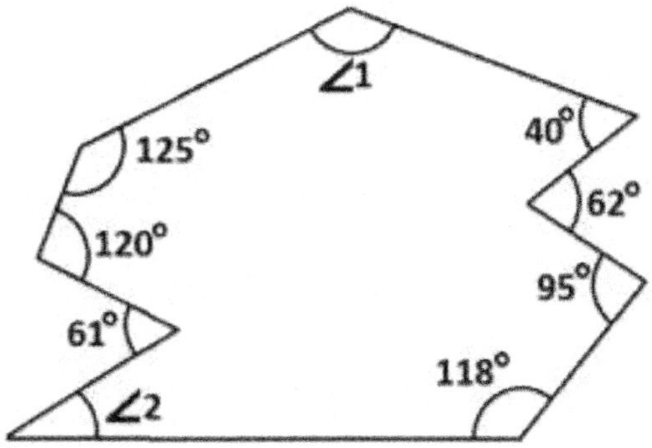

Sample

$\angle 1 = 135°$ $\angle 2 = ?$

Solution

$n = 9$

$(n-2)180° = (9-2)180° = 1260°$

interior $\angle$ at $\angle 61° = 360° - 61° = 299°$

interior $\angle$ at $\angle 62° = 360° - 62° = 298°$

Sum of known angles = 1230°

$\angle 2 = 1260° - 1230° = \underline{30°}$

Questions

	∠1	∠2
1.	123°	
2.	125°	
3.	131°	
4.	133°	

5. Given the following figure solve for the missing value(s).

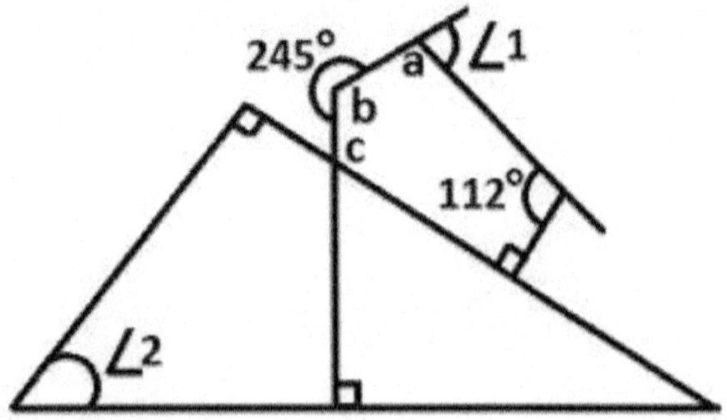

Sample

$\angle 1 = 77°$ $\angle 2 = ?$

Solution

$\angle a = 180° - 77° = \underline{103°}$

$\angle b = 360° - 245° = \underline{115°}$

$(n-2)180° = (5-2)180° = \underline{540°}$

$\angle c = 540° - (103 + 112 + 90 + 115)° = \underline{120°}$

$(n-2)180° = (4-2)180° = \underline{360°}$

$\angle 2 = 360° - (90 + 120 + 90)° = \underline{\underline{60°}}$

Questions

	$\angle 1$	$\angle 2$
1.	**71°**	
2.	**73°**	
3.	**75°**	
4.	**76°**	

6. **Given the following figure, solve for the missing value(s).**

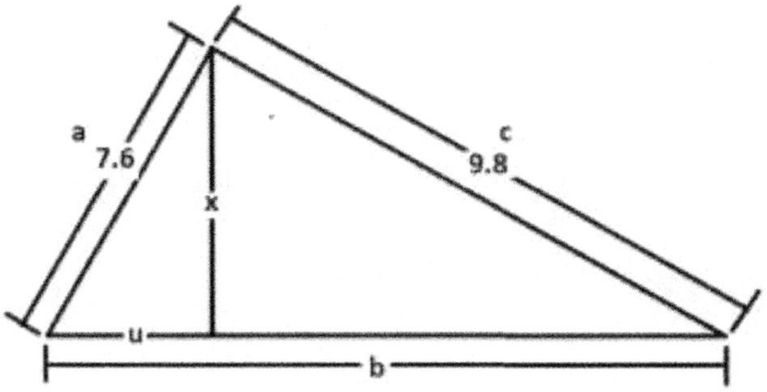

This question uses the formula for interior projection.

$$u = \frac{a^2 + b^2 - c^2}{2b}$$

Sample

$b = 12.4 \quad x = ?$

Solution

Find u first and then x.

$$u = \frac{a^2 + b^2 - c^2}{2b} = \frac{7.6^2 + 12.4^2 - 9.8^2}{2x12.4} = 4.656451613$$

$$u^2 + x^2 = a^2$$

$$x = \sqrt{a^2 - u^2} = \sqrt{7.6^2 - 4.656451613^2} = \underline{\underline{6.0065}}$$

Questions

	b	u	x
1.	12.1		
2.	11.8		
3.	10.9		
4.	10.6		

7. Given the following figure, solve for the missing value(s).

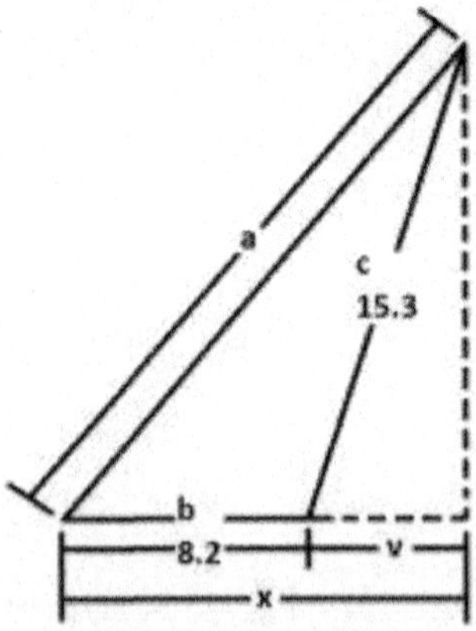

This question uses the exterior projection formula.

$$v = \frac{a^2 - b^2 - c^2}{2b}$$

Sample

$a = 18.917 \quad x = ?$

Solution

Find v first and then x.

$$v = \frac{18.917^2 - 8.2^2 - 15.3^2}{2x8.2} = 3.446517622$$

$$x = 8.2 + v = \underline{\underline{11.647}}$$

Questions

	a	v	x
1.	21.611		
2.	20.998		
3.	19.061		
4.	19.240		

8. Given the following figure, solve for the missing value(s).

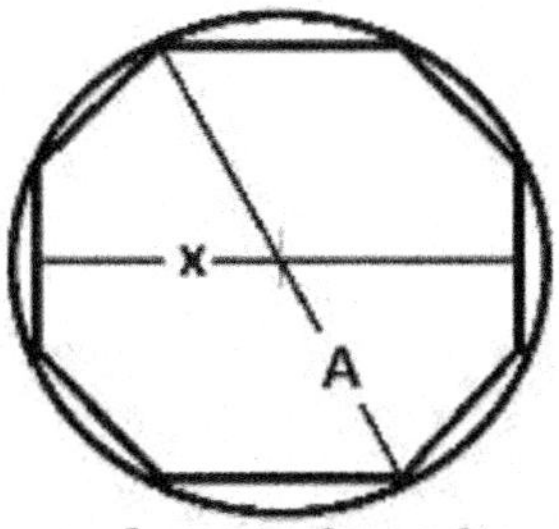

x = face to face distance
A = Diameter

Note: The side of an inscribed regular hexagon has the same length as the radius.

The easy formulas for this situation are:

$$x = \frac{\sqrt{3}}{2}A \qquad \text{or}$$

$$A = \frac{2}{\sqrt{3}}x$$

Sample if A=4.875, find x.

$$x = \frac{\sqrt{3}}{2}(4.875) = 4.221873843 = \underline{\underline{4.2219}}$$

Questions

	A	X		x	A
1 a	2.17		b.	5.25	
2 a	4.75		b.	5.16	
3 a	3.15		b.	5.76	
4 a	2.66		b.	6.09	

Block 3 Review

1. Trigonometric Functions
Standard Right Triangle and Labelling

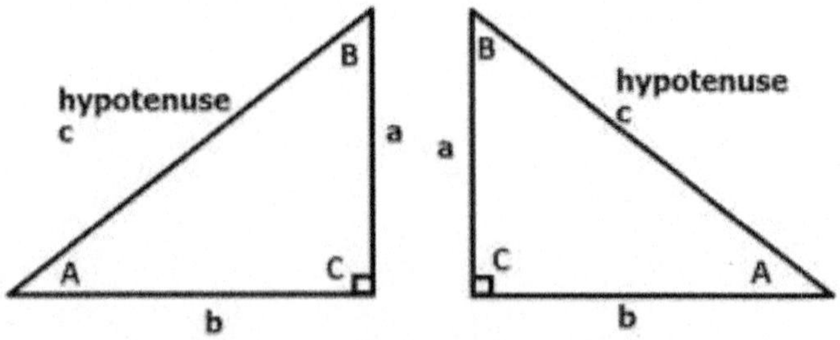

Pythagorean Theorem (P theory) - $c^2 = a^2 + b^2$

Basic Trig Ratios

$$\sin\theta = \frac{opposite}{hypotenuse}$$

$$\cos\theta = \frac{adjacent}{hypotenuse}$$

$$\tan\theta = \frac{opposite}{adjacent}$$

In Blocks 1 and 2, we looked at the idea of similar triangles. The trig ratios are simply another way to examine similar triangles.
For example

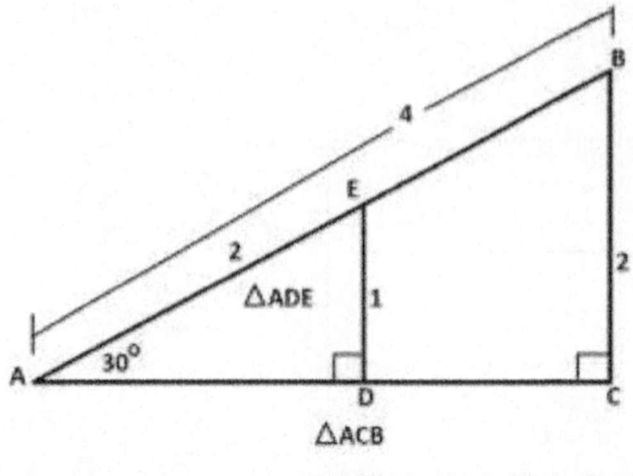

$\triangle ADE \equiv \triangle ACB$

$$\frac{DE}{AE} \equiv \frac{BC}{AB}$$

$$\frac{1}{2} \equiv \frac{2}{4}$$

Both share $\underline{\underline{\sin 30^\circ}}$

In fact no matter how many triangles are added, all will share the same angle with the same ratio of the *opposite side* to the *hypotenuse.*

A (long dead) mathematician referred to this special ratio as a *sine function* and the rest as they say is history. From the illustration above, it can be seen that regardless of the size of the triangle that $\sin 30^\circ \equiv 0.5$.

This ratio then along with the cosine and tangent ratios, allow us to solve any right angle triangle for missing sides and or angles.

Note:

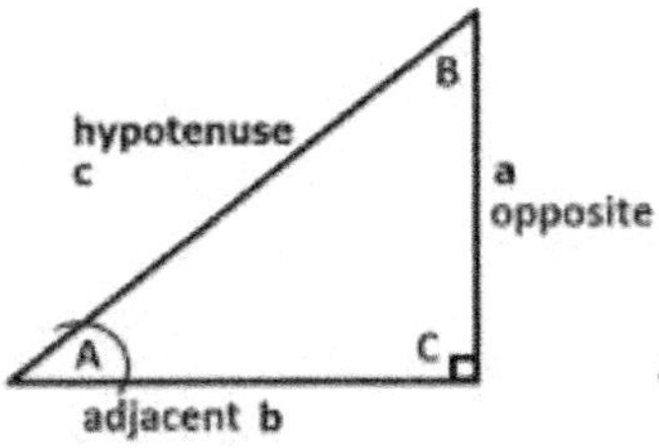

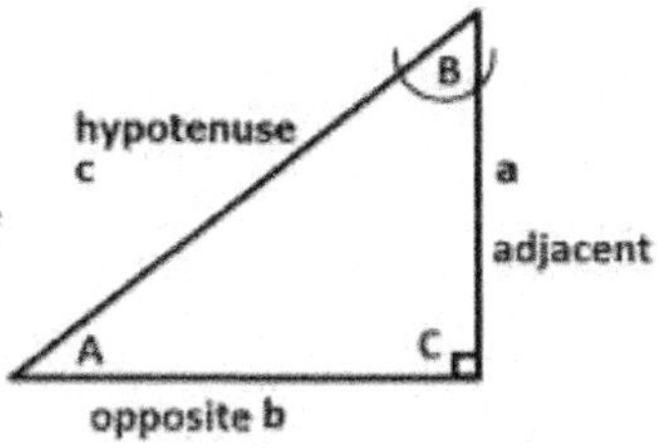

Based on where your angle is located will change where the 'opposite' and 'adjacent' sides are located.

Pythagorean Theorem Worksheet 1

Use the following illustration as a guide.

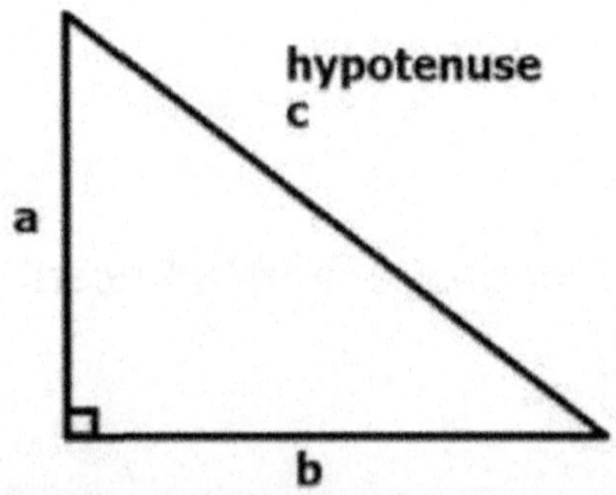

Solve for the missing side, three decimal places (nearest thousandths).

Problem #	Side a	Side b	Side c
1	3	4	
2	5		7.810
3		26	42.8
4	11	12	
5	75		125
6	50		92.649
7		24	33.242
8		14.23	17.73
9	8.99	10.05	
10		27.19	34.355
11	11.3125	14.5	
12		7.375	10.5
13	8.5		17.75
14		14.875	21.625
15		50.375	75.8125

$$c = \sqrt{a^2 + b^2} \quad a = \sqrt{c^2 - b^2} \quad b = \sqrt{c^2 - a^2}$$

Trigonometry Sine Ratio Worksheet 1

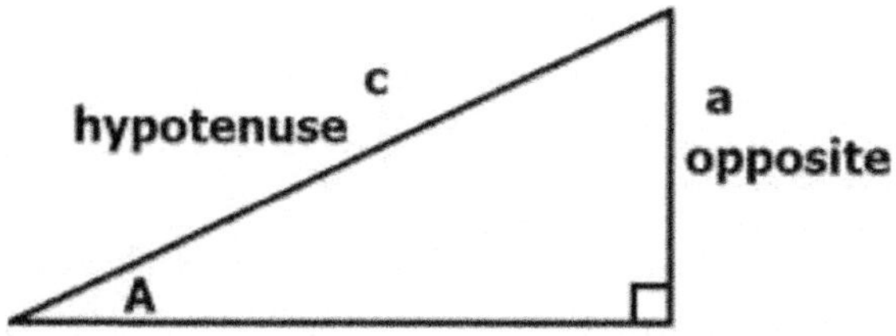

Solve for the angle or side, DMS for angles and 3 decimal places for sides.

Problem #	Side a	Side c	Angle A
1	3	5	
2	5	7.810	
3	34	42.8	
4	11	16.279	
5	75	125	
6		92.649	32°39'41"
7		33.242	43°46'49"
8		17.73	36°37'11"
9		13.484	41°48'50"
10		34.355	37°40'52"
11	11.3125		37°57'36"
12	7.474		45°22'56"
13	8.5		28°36'43"
14	15.696		46°32'16"
15	56.656		48°21'31"

Converting DMS to decimal

36°52'12"

$$36+\left(\frac{52}{60}\right)+\left(\frac{12}{3600}\right)$$

36.87°

$$\sin\angle A=\frac{opp}{hyp}=\frac{a}{c} \qquad a=c\cdot\sin\angle A \qquad c=\frac{a}{\sin\angle A}$$

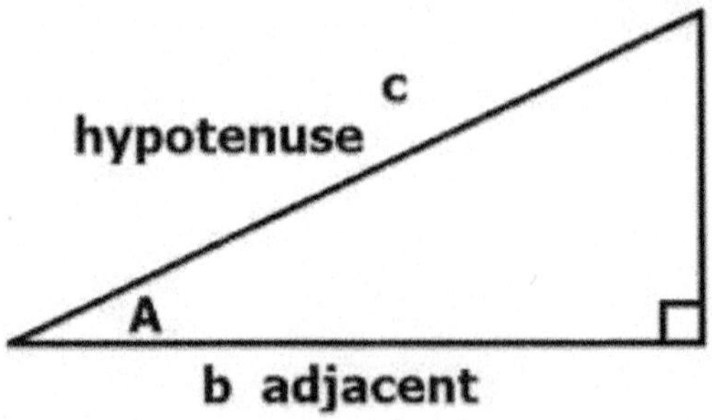

Solve for the angle or side, DMS for angles and 3 decimal places for sides.

Problem #	Side b	Side c	Angle A
1	4	5	
2	6	7.810	
3	26	42.8	
4	12	16.279	
5	100	125	
6		92.649	32°39'41"
7		33.242	43°46'49"
8		17.73	36°37'11"
9		13.484	41°48'50"
10		34.355	37°40'52"
11	14.5		37°57'36"
12	7.375		45°22'56"
13	15.582		28°36'43"
14	14.875		46°32'16"
15	50.375		48°21'31"

Converting DMS to decimal

$$36°52'12''$$

$$36+\left(\frac{52}{60}\right)+\left(\frac{12}{3600}\right)$$

$$36.87°$$

$$\cos\angle A=\frac{adj}{hyp}=\frac{b}{c} \qquad b=c\cdot\cos\angle A \qquad c=\frac{b}{\cos\angle A}$$

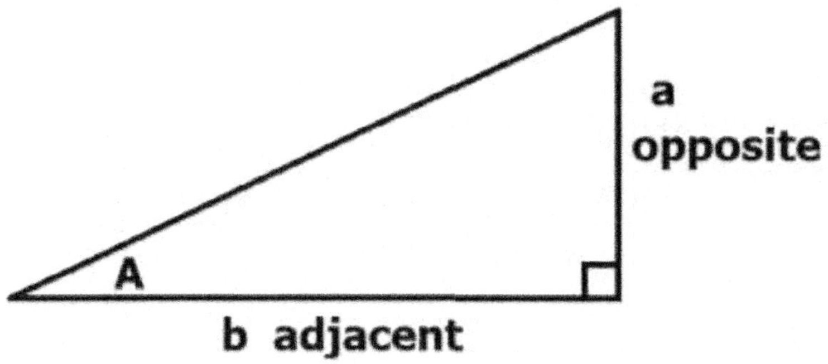

Solve for the angle or side, DMS for angles and 3 decimal places for sides.

Problem #	Side a	Side b	Angle A
1	3	4	
2	5	6	
3	33.998	26	
4	11	12	
5	75	100	
6		78	32°39'41"
7		24	43°46'49"
8		14.23	36°37'11"
9		10.05	41°48'50"
10		27.19	37°40'52"
11	11.3125		37°57'36"
12	7.474		45°22'56"
13	8.5		28°36'43"
14	15.696		46°32'16"
15	56.656		48°21'31"

$$\tan\angle A = \frac{opp}{adj} = \frac{a}{b} \qquad a = b \cdot \tan\angle A \qquad b = \frac{a}{\tan\angle A}$$

Pythagorean Theorem and Trig Functions Worksheet 2

Complete the table below. Angles are in DMS to the nearest second and sides are accurate to three (3) decimal places.

	Side a	Side b	Side c	Angle A	Angle B
1			35.000cm		48.0°
2			42.600cm	35.0°	
3	4.320m			69.0°	
4		8.370cm			54.0°
5	56.800cm				25.2°
6		28.500cm		75.4°	
7	1.650m			42°15′	
8		3.750m			64°24′
9	4.000cm	7.000cm			
10	5.000cm	8.000cm			
11	4.600cm	6.900cm			
12	1.500m	7.500m			
13		35.700m	41.300m		
14	85.600m		101m		
15	24.125in		45.752in		

$$c^2 = a^2 + b^2$$

$$\sin\angle = \frac{opp}{hyp} \quad \cos\angle = \frac{adj}{hyp} \quad \tan\angle = \frac{opp}{adj}$$

The angle value was left blank since it can be either ∠A or ∠B.

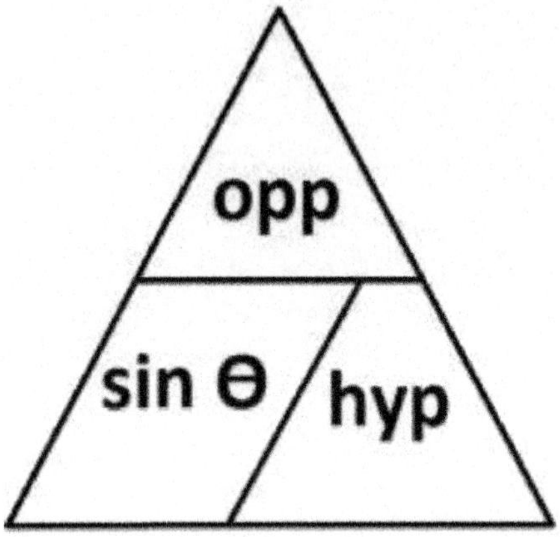

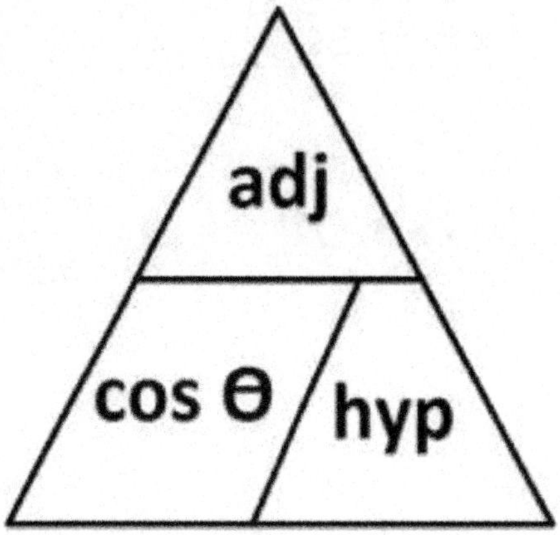

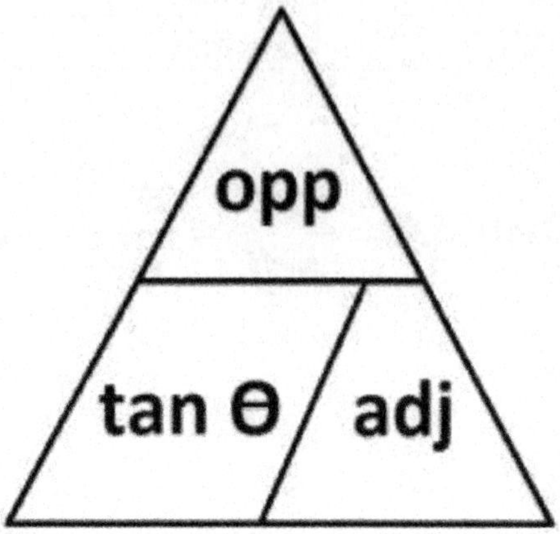

The above may help you with the trig formulas.

The applications that follow will show how these ratios and the p theory are used.

Sine Bar

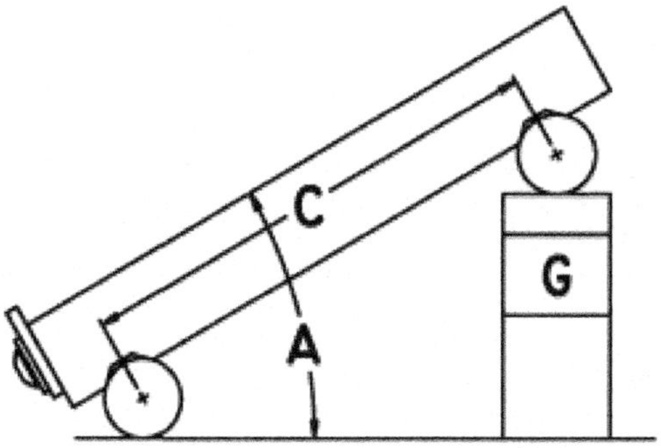

'C' refers to the fixed length of the sine bar, usually 5" or 10" (hypotenuse)

'G' refers to the gage blocks that are stacked to match the height (opposite)

'A' refers to the angle that is required.

This represents then the application of the sine function, hence the name 'sine' bar.

The most common application is to find the angle, so:

$$\sin\theta = \frac{opp}{hyp}$$

$$\therefore \theta = 2^{nd} \sin\left(\frac{opp}{hyp}\right)$$

Sample: A 10" sine bar rests on gage blocks that are 3.75" high. What is the angle of the sine bar?

$$\theta = 2^{nd} \sin\left(\frac{opp}{hyp}\right) = 2^{nd} \sin\left(\frac{3.75}{10}\right) = 22.02431284 = \underline{\underline{22°01'28''}}$$

Sample: A 10" sine bar is at an angle of 35°. What is the height of the gage blocks?

$$\sin\theta = \frac{opp}{hyp}$$

$$\sin 35° = \frac{opp}{10}$$

$$opp = 10 \cdot \sin 35° = 5.735764364 = \underline{\underline{5.74''}}$$

Sample: A sine bar makes an angle of 44° on a stack of gage blocks 6.947" in height.

What is the length of the sine bar to the nearest inch?

$$\sin 44^\circ = \frac{6.947}{hyp}$$

$$hyp = \frac{6.947}{\sin 44^\circ} = 10.00059928 = \underline{\underline{10"}}$$

Tapers and wedges

Wedge

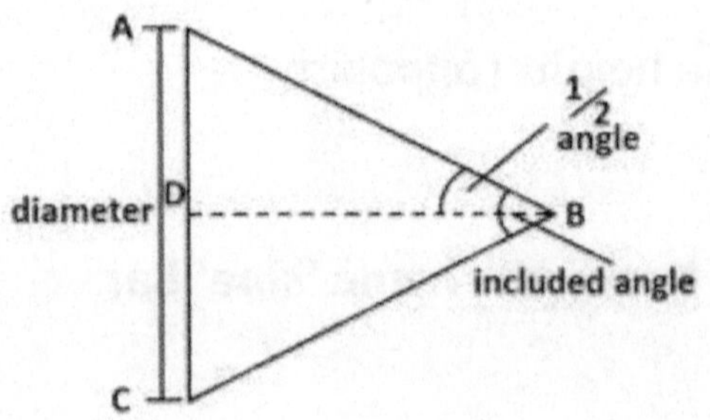

Note: $\angle ABD = \frac{1}{2}\angle ABC$ and $\overline{AD} = \frac{1}{2}\overline{AC}$ **The length** $\overline{DB}$ **may also be given. These values form a tangent ratio and so this is the ratio used to solve wedge problems.**

Tapers

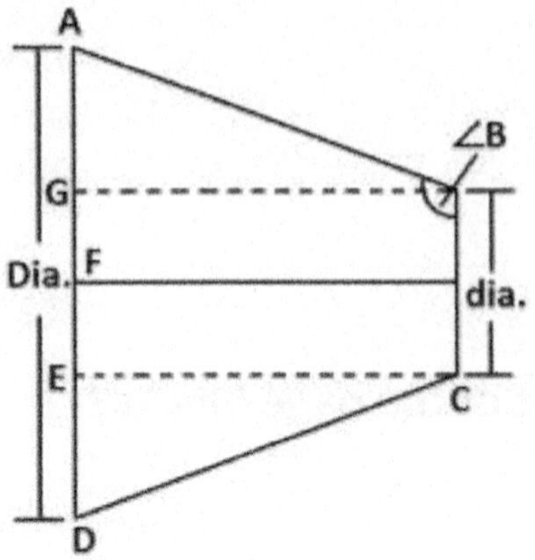

small diameter= $\overline{BC}$

large dia.= $\overline{AD}$

change in small dia.= $\overline{AG} + \overline{ED}$

included angle = $\angle ABG + \angle DCE$

$\angle B = \angle ABG + 90^\circ$

SAMPLES FOR BOTH FOLLOW.

Wedge Sample questions

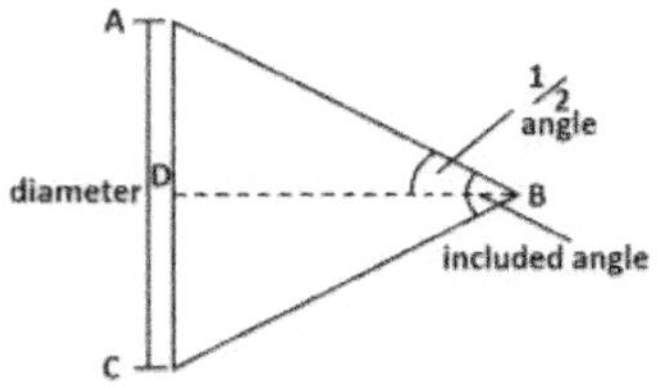

Sample 1:

Given: $\angle ABC = 34^\circ,\ \overline{BD} = 6",\quad dia. = ?$

$$\angle ABD = \frac{34}{2} = 17^\circ$$

$$\tan 17^\circ = \frac{\overline{AD}}{6"}$$

$$\overline{AD} = 6 \cdot \tan 17^\circ = 1.834384089$$

$$\overline{AC} = 2x\overline{AD} = \underline{\underline{3.6688"}}$$

Sample 2:

Given: $\overline{AC} = 5", \overline{BD} = 8",\quad$ included angle=?

$$\tan\theta = \frac{2.5}{8}$$

$$\theta = 2^{nd} \tan\left(\frac{2.5}{8}\right) = 17.35402464^\circ$$

$$2\theta = 34.70804927^\circ = \underline{\underline{34^\circ 42' 29"}}$$

Sample 3:

Given: included angle=$28^\circ 04',\ \overline{AC} = 5",\quad \overline{BD} = ?$

$$\theta = \frac{28^\circ 04'}{2} = 14^\circ 02' = 14.03333333^\circ$$

$$\tan 14.03333333^\circ = \frac{2.5}{\overline{BD}}$$

$$\overline{BD} = \frac{2.5}{\tan 14.03333333^\circ} = 10.00215907 = \underline{\underline{10"}}$$

Taper Sample Questions

Sample 1: Find the included angle.

Given: $\overline{BC} = 4"$, $\overline{AD} = 7"$, $\overline{BG} = 12"$

$7" - 4" = 3"$, $\frac{3"}{2} = 1.5" = \overline{AG}$

$\theta = 2^{nd} \tan\left(\frac{1.5}{12}\right)$

$\theta = 7.125016349°$

$2\theta = 14.2500327° = \underline{\underline{14°15'}}$

Sample 2: Find the large diameter of the taper

Given: $\overline{GB} = 10.5"$, $\overline{BC} = 3"$, included angle=2θ=24°

$\frac{24}{2} = 12° = \angle ABG$ $\overline{AG} = opp$

$\overline{AG} = 10.5 \tan 12°$

$= 2.231843898"$

$2x\overline{AG} = 4.463687795 = 4.464"$

$\overline{AD} = 3" + 4.464" = \underline{\underline{7.464"}}$

Sample 3: Find the small diameter of the taper

Given: $\overline{AD} = 4"$, $\overline{GB} = 7"$, included angle $2\theta = 20°$

$\overline{AG} = opp$

$opp = 7" x \tan 10° = 1.2343$

$x2 = 2.4686$

small dia. $\overline{BC} = 4" - 2.4686" = \underline{\underline{1.5314"}}$

Sample 4: Determine the taper per foot (TPF)

TPF describes the change in diameter per foot (can also be TPI {taper per inch})

Given: $\overline{AD} = 7"$, $\overline{BC} = 4"$

$TPF =$ large dia. - small dia.

$TPF = \overline{AD} - \overline{BC} = 7 - 4 = 3$

$TPF = \underline{\underline{3"}}$

Center to Center Bolt Hole distances

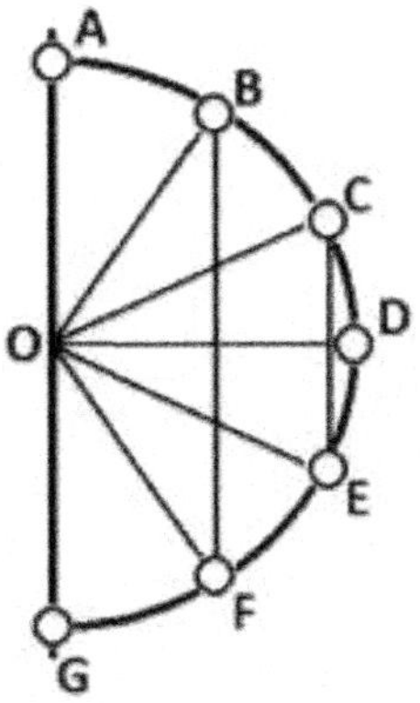

Sample 1

The radius of the circle is 5", ∠COE is 60°, what is the distance between C and E?

$\angle COE = 60°, \angle COD = 30°$

$\sin 30° = \dfrac{opp}{5"}$

$opp = 5 \cdot \sin 30° = 2.5"$

$\overline{CE}$ is two times this distance

$\overline{CE} = 5"$

Sample 2

The center to center distance from C to E is 3.4202 and the radius is 5".

What is ∠COE?

$\dfrac{3.4202}{2} = 1.7101$

$\sin\theta = \left(\dfrac{1.7101}{5}\right)$

$\theta = 2^{nd} \sin\left(\dfrac{1.7101}{5}\right) = 20°$

$\angle COE = 2x20° = 40°$

Sample 3

Radius=5″, $\overline{CE}$ =5.4202″, ∠COE=40°

What is the distance from O to chord CE?

$$\cos 20^\circ = \frac{adj}{5''}$$

This could also have been solved with P theory.

$$adj = 5 \cdot \cos 20^\circ = 4.6985''$$

ANSWERS TO THE QUESTIONS

Blocks 1-3 Answer Summary

Page 15

Multiply							
1.	3480	**2.**	58028	**3.**	142528	**4.**	408
5.	686	**6.**	21.165	**7.**	9.6252	**8.**	97.578125
9.	4.00390625	**10.**	4				
Divide							
1.	96	**2.**	612	**3.**	148	**4.**	392
5.	71	**6.**	124.25	**7.**	178.5	**8.**	234.75
9.	24.375	**10.**	321.625				

Page 19

Shop Fractions

Addition							
1.	$1\frac{3}{4}$	**2.**	$\frac{25}{64}$	**3.**	$2\frac{1}{8}$	**4.**	$\frac{5}{6}$
5.	$\frac{21}{64}$	**6.**	$1\frac{21}{32}$	**7.**	$1\frac{7}{16}$	**8.**	$1\frac{3}{64}$
9.	$\frac{3}{32}$	**10.**	$1\frac{5}{64}$	**11.**	$2\frac{1}{16}$	**12.**	$1\frac{9}{64}$
13.	$1\frac{21}{32}$						
Subtraction							
14.	$\frac{3}{8}$	**15.**	$\frac{39}{64}$	**16.**	$\frac{1}{4}$	**17.**	$\frac{3}{16}$
18.	$\frac{3}{64}$	**19.**	$\frac{9}{16}$	**20.**	$\frac{17}{32}$	**21.**	$\frac{27}{64}$
22.	$\frac{19}{64}$	**23.**	$\frac{21}{64}$	**24.**	$\frac{45}{64}$	**25.**	$\frac{1}{4}$
26.	$\frac{29}{64}$						

Page 25

Multiply							
1.	$\frac{5}{16}$	**2.**	$\frac{39}{256}$	**3.**	$\frac{15}{64}$	**4.**	$\frac{3}{8}$
5.	$\frac{17}{2048}$	**6.**	$\frac{65}{128}$	**7.**	$\frac{65}{256}$	**8.**	$\frac{105}{2048}$
9.	$\frac{1}{256}$	**10.**	$\frac{91}{256}$	**11.**	$\frac{65}{512}$	**12**	$\frac{663}{2048}$
13.	$\frac{15}{64}$	**14.**	$1\frac{1}{4}$	**15.**	$1\frac{1}{16}$	**16.**	$1\frac{2}{3}$
17.	$1\frac{1}{6}$	**18.**	$8\frac{1}{2}$	**19.**	$1\frac{3}{10}$	**20.**	$1\frac{7}{13}$
21.	$4\frac{2}{7}$	**22.**	$\frac{32}{35}$	**23.**	$2\frac{2}{13}$	**24.**	$3\frac{1}{13}$
25.	$1\frac{19}{39}$	**26.**	$8\frac{8}{11}$				

Page 28

Fractions to decimals

1.	**0.25**	**2.**	**0.5**	**3.**	**0.75**
4.	**0.3125**	**5.**	**0.875**	**6.**	**1.125**
7.	**2.25**	**8.**	**3.03125**	**9.**	**7.125**
10.	**12.109375**				

Page 29

Decimals to fractions

1.	$\frac{3}{16}$	**2.**	$\frac{3}{8}$	**3.**	$\frac{11}{32}$
4.	$\frac{7}{16}$	**5.**	$\frac{1}{8}$	**6.**	$2\frac{1}{4}$
7.	$11\frac{1}{8}$	**8.**	$24\frac{3}{8}$	**9.**	$9\frac{7}{16}$
10.	$17\frac{5}{8}$				

Page 35 Percentages Practice Sheet Answers

TYPE 1 Finding Part when Rate and Base is Given

1.	24.06	2.	139.202	3.	49.0448
4.	588.024	5.	61.87	6.	2.7376
7.	3.87725	8.	23.381325	9.	215.5761375
10.	1127.838536				

TYPE 2 Finding the Base (Whole) when the Part and Rate is Given

	Part	Base (Whole)	Rate %
1.	16	800	2
2.	12	48	25
3.	40	228.57	17.5
4.	8.125	50	16 ¼
5.	354	600	59
6.	16.56	72	23
7.	31.5	90	35
8.	72	600	12
9.	418.95	735	57
10.	336.2	820	41

Page 36

TYPE 3 Finding Rate when Part and Base is Given

	Part	Base (Whole)	Percent
1.	4	16	25
2.	10	25	40
3.	27	60	45
4.	11.6	16	72.5
5.	9	27	$33\frac{1}{3}$
6.	18	270	$6\frac{2}{3}$
7.	63	64	98.4
8.	15	32	46.9
9.	12	64	18.8
10.	2.5	200	1.3

Fill in the Table

Question	Tolerance	Maximum Value	Minimum Value
1.	$\frac{1}{8}$"	$25\frac{7}{32}$"	$24\frac{31}{32}$
2.	$\frac{1}{32}$"	**12.40625"**	**12.34375"**
3.	**0.006"**	2.818"	**2.806"**
4.	**0.007mm**	**289.012mm**	$288.998mm$
5.	$0.1mm$	**62.14mm**	**61.94mm**

Fill in the Table

Question	Maximum Value	Mean	Minimum Value	Tolerance
1.	$28\frac{1}{32}$	28	$27\frac{31}{32}$	$\pm\frac{1}{32}$
2.	17.5515	**17.504**	17.4565	**±0.0475**
3.	$2\frac{15}{16}$	$2\frac{7}{8}$	$2\frac{13}{16}$	$\pm\frac{1}{16}$
4.	**21.4375**	21.0625	**20.6875**	±0.375
5.	285.0625	**285**	284.9375	**±0.0625**

Page 38

1.	4	**2.**	-10	**3.**	-10	**4.**	10
5.	21	**6.**	-50	**7.**	-21	**8.**	-1/4
9.	21	**10.**	4	**11.**	-7	**12.**	-3

Page 41 & 42 Degrees, DMS and operations

ANSWERS

	DD	DMS
1	27.3475°	27°20'51"
2	33.7894°	33°47'22"
3	45.01345°	45°0'48"
4	78.71492°	78°42'54"
5	12.112985°	12°06'47"
6	22.63459°	22°38'05"
7	10.985432°	10°59'08"
8	17.56473°	17°33'53"
9	25.375°	25°22'30"
10	61.0375°	61°02'15"

	DMS	DD
1	48°21'09"	48.3525°
2	24°16'58"	24.2828°
3	71°33'12"	71.553°
4	43°15'15"	43.25417°
5	12°55'48"	12.93°
6	32°19'01"	32.31694°
7	51°31'44"	51.528°
8	13°45'56"	13.7656°
9	77°38'11"	77.63639°
10	53°27'45"	53.4625°

1. 45°16'54" + 17°43'17" = **63°00'11"**

2. 115°23'41" + 62°15'23" = **177°39'04"**

3. 63°22'01" + 21°16'25" = **84°38'26"**

4. 56°20'32" + 21°34'18" = **77°54'50"**

5. 71°42'21" + 33°51'34" = **105°33'55"**

1. 45°16'54" – 17°43'17" = **27°33'37"**

2. 115°23'41" – 62°15'23" = **53°08'18"**

3. 63°22'01" – 21°16'25" = **42°05'36"**

4. 56°20'32" – 21°34'18" = **34°46'14"**

5. 71°42'21" – 33°51'34" = **37°50'47"**

Page 44

1.	85	**2.**	18	**3.**	25	**4.**	57	**5.**	46
6.	0	**7.**	26	**8.**	16	**9.**	-55	**10.**	78

Page 47

1.	64	**2.**	4	**3.**	1	**4.**	64	**5.**	15.625
6.	10	**7.**	4	**8.**	11	**9.**	10	**10.**	16

Page 51 Ratios/Proportions Answers

Direct Ratios

Question	Solution
1.	$\frac{27}{40} = \frac{x}{100} \to 40x = 2700 \to x = \frac{2700}{40} = \underline{\underline{67.5}}$
2.	75
3.	3
4.	3
5.	10
6.	342 lbs
7.	75,000 lbs
8.	134.78 kg
9.	9.375 kg
10.	60 welds

Page 52, 53 Indirect Ratios/Proportions

Question	Solution
1.	$\frac{2000}{B} = \frac{18"}{21"} \to 18B = 42000 \to B = \underline{\underline{2333 rpm}}$
2.	13.91 rpm
3.	0.48 Pa
4.	360 ml
5.	553.17 ml
6.	564.17 cm^3
7.	21.75 atm
8.	14.4"
9.	1687.5 rpm
10.	25 cm

Page 58

Conversions Practice

1.	657.5 yd	11.	6 015 m
2.	1 980 ft	12.	2.03 m
3.	6 541 m	13.	29 in
4.	8 689 g	14.	9.51 m
5.	40 920 ft	15.	3.219 km
6.	2 420 yd	16.	95 in
7.	605 m	17.	88.91 cm
8.	7.75 ft	18.	2.069 kg
9.	5.17 ft	19.	3 419.69 m
10.	140 mm	20.	7.62 m

Page 59

Area Volume Conversions

1.	3.875	11.	1.526
2.	206.45	12.	524.38
3.	1 161.288	13.	35 395.92
4.	29 728.97	14.	75 511.296
5.	32	15.	2.67
6.	7 989.66	16.	243 523.93
7.	27.59	17.	10.86
8.	300	18.	118.11
9.	2.083	19.	0.068
10.	1 550	20.	61 015.68

Page 74

Volume to weight ANSWERS

1.	3897.14 g = 3.90 kg
2.	1661.41 lbs
3.	2951.32 lbs
4.	12852 kg
5.	207570 kg
6.	
Plate A (x2)	7112
Plate B (x2)	4064
Plate C	3556
Tot. Vol.	14732 cm^3
Weight	115.65 kg

Page 75

1.	7797 kg
2.	1530.75 lbs
3.	1166.96 lbs
4.	16008.3 kg
5.	124875 kg
6.	
Tot Vol.	754 in^3
7.	
Tot Wt.	203.75 lbs – 217.92 lbs

Page 82

1.	$W = \frac{P-2L}{2} = 4cm$
2.	$h = \frac{2A}{b} = 7in$
3.	$r = \frac{C}{2\pi} = 5cm$
4.	**7.7175**
5.	$s = \frac{S}{\pi r} = 2.7559$
6.	$F = \frac{9C}{5} + 32 = 80.6°F$
7.	$B = \frac{2A}{H} - D = 20$
8.	$r = \sqrt{\frac{V}{\pi L}} = 15cm$

Page 83 – 90 Geometry Problems Answers

1.	#1	41°	2.	#1	9°		3.	#1	148°		4.	#1	42°
	#2	43°		#2	6°			#2	150°			#2	40°
	#3	49°		#3	2°			#3	156°			#3	34°
	#4	51°		#4	15°			#4	158°			#4	32°
5.	#1	66°	6.	#1	4.468	6.1478	7.	#1	10.104	18.304	8.	#1	1.8793
	#2	64°		#2	4.278	6.2816		#2	8.511	16.711		#2	4.1136
	#3	62°		#3	3.694	6.6418		#3	5.053	13.253		#3	2.7279
	#4	61°		#4	3.494	6.749		#4	4.198	12.398		#4	2.3036

Page 93

Pythagorean and Trig Worksheets ANSWERS

Prob. #	Side a	Side b	Side c
1			5.00
2		6.00	
3	33.998		
4			16.279
5		100	
6		78	
7	23		
8	10.576		
9			13.484
10	21		
11			18.391
12	7.474		
13		15.582	
14	15.696		
15	56.656		

Page 94

Prob. #	Side a	Side c	Angle A
1			36°52'12"
2			39°48'26"
3			52°35'53"
4			42°30'36"
5			36°52'12"
6	50		
7	23		
8	10.576		
9	8.990		
10	21		
11		18.391	
12		10.5	
13		17.75	
14		21.625	
15		75.812	

Page 95

Prob. #	Side b	Side c	Angle A
1			36°52'12"
2			39°48'26"
3			52°35'53"
4			42°30'36"
5			36°52'12"
6	77.999		
7	24		
8	14.230		
9	10.05		
10	27.189		
11		18.391	
12		10.5	
13		17.75	
14		21.625	
15		75.813	

Page 96

Prob. #	Side a	Side b	Angle A
1			36°52'12"
2			39°48'26"
3			52°35'53"
4			42°30'36"
5			36°52'12"
6	50		
7	23		
8	10.578		
9	8.99		
10	21		
11		14.5	
12		7.375	
13		15.582	
14		14.875	
15		50.375	

Page 97

	Side a	Side b	Side c	Angle A	Angle B
1	23.419	26.010		42°	
2	24.434	34.896			55°
3		1.658	4.627		21°
4	6.08		10.35	36°	
5		26.73	62.77	64°48'0"	25.2°
6	109.413		113.064		14°36'0"
7		1.817	2.454		47°15'0"
8	1.797		4.158	25°36'0"	
9			8.062	29°44'0"	60°16'0"
10			9.434	32°0'19"	57°59'41"
11			8.293	33°41'24"	56°18'36"
12			7.649	11°18'36"	78°41'24"
13	20.765			30°11'06"	59°48'54"
14		53.606		57°56'36"	32°3'24"
15		38.875		31°49'23"	58°10'37"

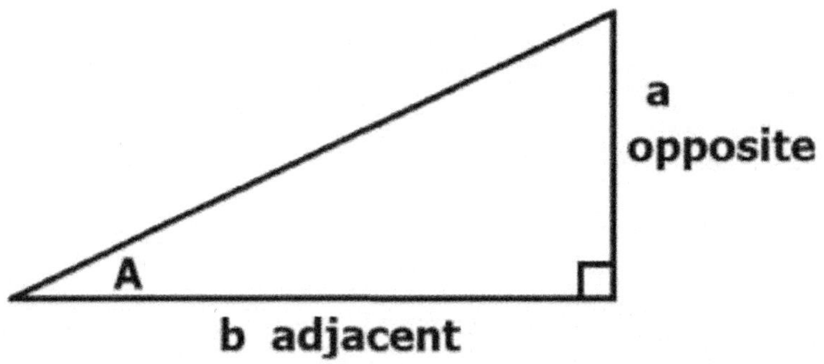

Note that the table above was solved with the above Angle A position.

Printed in Great Britain
by Amazon

37868344R00066